Dreaming up America

dreaming up America

RUSSELL BANKS

SEVEN STORIES PRESS

New York · London · Melbourne · Toronto

SEVEN STORIES PRESS
140 Watts Street
New York, NY 10013
www.sevenstories.com

In Canada:
Publishers Group Canada
559 College Street, Suite 402, Toronto, ON M6G 1A9 Canada

Library of Congress Cataloging-in-Publication Data

Banks, Russell, 1940-
Dreaming up America / Russell Banks.
—Seven Stories Press 1st ed.
p. cm.
ISBN 978-1-58322-838-8 (hardcover)
1. National characteristics, American.
2. United States—Civilization.
3. United States—History.
I. Title.
E169.1.B2218 2008
973—dc22
2008011099

Book design by Pollen, New York
Image research by David A. Zuckerman

College professors may order examination copies
of Seven Stories Press titles for a free
six-month trial period. To order, visit
www.sevenstories.com/textbook or fax on school
letterhead to (212) 226-1411.

Printed in the United States of America

9 8 7 6 5 4 3 2 1

contents

List of iLLustrations

Author's Note

PERHAPS THIS should be called a "speaker's note," since *Dreaming Up America* began as a spoken text and not a written one. It was occasioned by an invitation to me and my fellow American novelist and friend, Jim Harrison, from a French documentary filmmaker, Jean-Michel Meurice. He wanted us to play talking heads in a film he was making for the French television channel, Arte. The film, Monsieur Meurice explained, was to be about American history as told by American cinema—from *The Birth of a Nation* to *Blackhawk Down*. Harrison and I were to construct a counter-narrative and between us provide a two-hour corrective to the version of American history that French people were most familiar with, that is, the cinematic version. Its title was to be *Amérique notre histoire.*

Jean-Michel Meurice is a charming man who speaks better English than either Harrison or I speak French, and we agreed to participate in this project, not because we were particularly eager to correct the French view of "notre histoire," but because he invited us next time we were in France to visit his home on the Mediterranean near Toulouse, where he promised to cook his legendary bouillabaisse using mussels and oysters harvested that very morning. He also appealed to our literary egos by insisting that our versions of American history, as novelists, would be superior to any historians' versions. We did not disabuse him of this notion.

It would take only a single day of our time, he added, and he would bring his crew to the United States and film us in our homes, me in Saratoga Springs, New York, Harrison in Montana. We would be seated against a blue screen, while Jean-Michel himself stood off camera and asked each of us separately a series of questions that were designed to let us ruminate and, if we wished, to fulminate on specific aspects of American history. Clips from the films were to be cut into the documentary later. His questions would be edited out, à la Ken Burns, so that Harrison and I would appear to be sitting across from each other at a table waxing garrulous, while scenes from *Across the Wild Missouri,*

Captain Blood, and *Sergeant York* played behind us. "You may digress, if you wish, and bring to the subject whatever comes to your mind," he said. Not a wise invitation to a novelist, when you've only got two hours of film time available.

On a raw morning in February, Jean-Michel and his crew arrived in Saratoga Springs and for eleven hours filmed my responses to his brief, open-ended questions. Film is an ongoing dream, and history is another kind of dream, regressive, perhaps, like memory. In this case, both dreams were generated by the same reality, America, and the collision between them stimulated me more than I had anticipated. The typed transcript of my responses to Jean-Michel's questions turned out to be nearly one hundred pages long, which, using a French voice-over, he ultimately edited down to about a half-hour of film time.

My French publisher, Marie-Catherine Vacher at Actes Sud, read the entire transcript and had it translated by Pierre Furlan, who translates most of my fiction into French. In October 2006, in conjunction with Arte Editions, it was published as *Amérique notre histoire*, released at the same time as Jean-Michel's documentary. The book and the film were well received, and as there are now several other translated versions of the book in the works—Spanish, Italian, and so on, there seemed no reason not to publish it in the original English. I'm grateful to Dan Simon and his Seven

Author's Note

Stories Press for their willingness to take it on. For the American edition, I expanded on some of the ideas and eliminated some of the redundancies, but not all, since we wanted to preserve the flavor of a spoken text. Which brings me back to my opening remark, that this is a speaker's note as much as it is an author's note. I must beg the reader's indulgence, therefore, of certain stylistic infelicities that would pass unnoticed if uttered by a talking head in a documentary film, especially one that lasted the nearly eleven hours that it would take to speak the entire text. Perhaps Jean-Michel Meurice did me a favor by leaving all but a half-hour of the transcript on the cutting-room floor. If so, then I direct you to the DVD of *Amérique notre histoire.*

Dreaming Up America

MAP OF NORTH
AMERICA, 1697

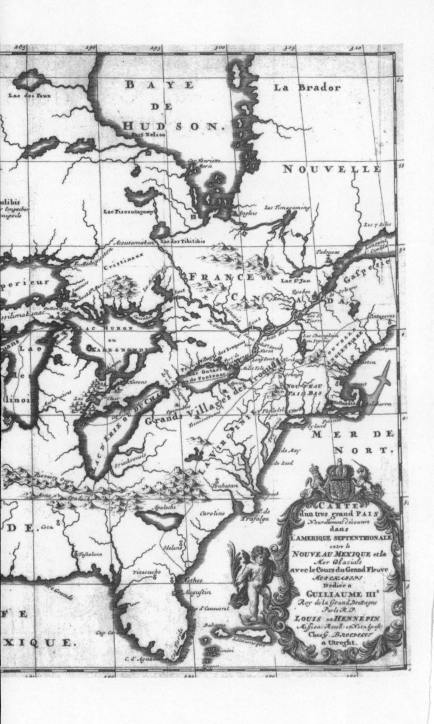

THE EARLIEST SIGNS OF AN AMERICAN SENSIBILITY

BEFORE WE start to think or talk seriously about our American values, there are a few things I want to say about the first colonists, the first Europeans residing in North America. We have to remember that they came from different parts of Europe and that they came to North America with very different ideas about what they wanted to do here. The English colonists came to New England in search of religious freedom, with a fundamentalist Protestant vision of their own mission and with their own religious and political agenda. The Dutch came to the area where I live—New York, Manhattan, the Hudson Valley—strictly for com-

1

mercial reasons, to fish and to trade for beaver and lumber, not for reasons of religion or freedom or politics. The Spanish sailed into the Caribbean, to Florida, to the coast of the Gulf of Mexico, and into Mexico for gold, and had no particular ambitions to make a community or colony.

There were all these different motives and very different values associated with each of them. At the very beginning of the colonization of America—which we'll do well to remember wasn't the same as the beginning of America, since the place these Europeans "discovered" was inhabited already—these differences between the English, the Dutch, and the Spanish established at the start a world of potential conflict between the spiritual intentions of those fleeing inhospitable European societies on the one hand, and the commercial ambitions of those seeking profitable opportunities on the other. Was America going to be a haven, a miraculous place where you could build a Protestant City on a Hill? Or was it a vast continent ripe for pillage and exploitation, a bottomless storehouse to loot for the enrichment of Europe—Spain, Holland, France, and England?

So when we speak of the values of the first colonists, we cannot lump them together. It depends on who we're talking about. *Which* colonists? And since for various reasons they grouped themselves together geographically, it also depends on *where* we're talking about. Is it the southern United States, the coastal regions along the Gulf of Mexico and the Caribbean? If so, the dominant values driving early settlement were coldly materialistic and exploitative. If we're talking about the middle colonies like Virginia, Maryland, New York, and Pennsylvania, then the dominant interests were more narrowly commercial: trading, fishing, lumber, tapping the region for its products. And in New England from the time of the earliest colonists, issues of religion and of creating a new spiritual haven were front and center, not simply the accouterments of commerce or exploitation.

Gradually, of course, those ambitions began to merge. In the South you saw materialist ambitions justified by religious and spiritual aspirations and principles. In New England you saw spiritual and religious ambitions begin to fade as the colonists seized the opportunity to exploit the region's natural resources economically. So that by the early eighteenth century enough blending had occurred for Americans, the colonists, to no longer think of themselves as Europeans. By then the braiding together of the two strands had begun to form a national culture, a shared sense of national values. But at bottom these were still conflicting values. And I think that as we move forward in this discussion we'll see the inherent conflict between those two sets of values come up again and again and again.

I spoke of the point at which the pioneers stopped feeling European. But I don't know that they ever felt

European as such. When they first arrived on our shores, their separate national identities were stronger than any single overarching European sense of identity. In the sixteenth and seventeenth centuries, the Spanish colonists felt Spanish more than they felt European. The French felt French more than European. And the English felt English, not at all European. So we have to make that distinction at the beginning. The question is, at what point did the English colonists stop feeling English? At what point did the Spanish colonists stop feeling Spanish, and the French stop feeling French? It didn't all happen at the same time. And what's interesting is that the types of governance that were established for each country's colonies helped determine how they identified themselves initially and the pace at which their new American identities evolved.

The English managed to set up administrative structures that provided a great deal of local autonomy, in New England particularly. And in Virginia and throughout all the English colonies, there were local legislative bodies, local governors and public officials who operated rather independently from the mother country, whereas the Spanish and the French still ruled much more closely from home. In Quebec and in the French colonies, for instance, and even in Maryland, which existed briefly as a French colony, and in Louisiana, when the French ruled, they ruled from home, as if their colonies were branch offices, whereas the English decentralized authority to a much greater extent, as if their colonies were franchises.

Therefore most New Englanders by the mid- to late seventeenth century, the 1680s and '90s, felt more American than English. They stopped feeling English much earlier than the French and Spanish stopped feeling French and Spanish. In Quebec, for instance, where even today they feel more French than Canadian, there's still that pull from the mother country, and I think this was also true at the time for the Spanish and the Dutch. It's an interesting question, but once again it shows us that you can't generalize about the early colonists unless you acknowledge their multiple places of origin. We don't just have one mother country. We have many dueling mothers who all play a significant role in creating us.

And of course African origins were very important in this period. There were vast numbers of Africans present from the start, in the South particularly, but throughout the colonies. After all, until the 1830s there were slaves in New England, slaves in New York and New Jersey. It wasn't just in the South that Americans owned slaves. So we have to consider the influence of African values, African culture. It's just below the surface at the start, necessarily so, but it's there. The African factor was profoundly operative, and it was influential to an extreme degree on the dominant white culture, especially in the South, so we have to acknowledge that strand, too. The very same culture that would have its flourishing in the twentieth century with the blues, with jazz, and in the visual and language arts, was already a force in the eighteenth century and especially throughout the nineteenth century when Africans made up a significant portion of the American population.

Was there an early form of the American Dream? I can't say there was *one* American Dream. There were several dreams to begin with. There was El Dorado, the City of Gold that Cortez and Pizarro dreamed of finding. And then there was Ponce de Leon's dream of the Fountain of Youth, where you could start life over again, and the New England Puritan dream of God's Protestant utopian City on a Hill, the New Jerusalem. There were at least three distinct dreams in the beginning.

The religious dream of the City on the Hill, where you could live a life that was pure and uninfected by European cosmopolitanism, was almost a pastoral dream, one in which you could become a natural human being living a holy life under the eye of God. And you could only do it here, in the New Jerusalem. You couldn't do it in corrupt old Europe. It was only possible in the New World.

The dream of the City of Gold, where you discovered untold wealth, was a dream of glory in the service of the Old World. You melted down the gold, poured it into bullion, and shipped it back to enrich the crowned heads of Europe. It was a powerful material dream, and it was this dream that became the model for the exploitation of the New World, although it was the least transformative of the three.

The dream of the Fountain of Youth may yet prove to be the strongest of the three, since it carries within it the sense of the new, the dream of starting over, of having a New Life. It's essentially the dream of being a child again, and it's the dream that persists more strongly than the other two and is today perhaps the most vivid of the three. We can think of there being three braided strands, or perhaps three mutually reinforcing dreams: one is of a place where a sinner can become virtuous, free from the decadence of the secular cosmopolitanism of old Europe; another is of a place where a poor man can become wealthy; and a third is of a place where a person can be born again.

The three together are much more powerful than any one of them alone. And they are there at the inception, at the very beginning of colonial America, side by side at first, specific to the three separate regions, but gradually merging. By the late seventeenth and early eighteenth centuries they come together, just as the colonies themselves begin to come together. As the northern colonies in New England begin to attach themselves to the middle colonies—New York, Pennsylvania, Maryland, Virginia—and then the southern colonies—

South Carolina, North Carolina, Georgia—begin to draw together, and as the English more or less achieve military and economic control and establish a kind of cultural hegemony across the eastern seaboard, you see the three dreams merge.

Forging America's idea of itself

AS AMERICANS from New England moved west into Ohio and Wisconsin and into the far northwestern territories, the first building they put up in every newly settled village was a white church with a steeple. The second building was the town hall, where everyone voted. In other words, the two pillars they carried with them were their form of representative government and along with that the notion that God was central to the community. The third building was the schoolhouse. The fourth was probably the bank. No brothels or saloons till much later, of course.

Religious fundamentalism and the idea of God are as central to our social and political organization as our vaunted democratic institutions. It has to do with the particular Protestant sects that settled in New England in the seventeenth century and made God central to the political organization there. It was not made central anywhere else—not by the French in Quebec and the north of New England, and not by the Spanish in Florida and the Caribbean. Catholic priests accompanied the Spanish and French colonists, yes, but they were not central to the political life in the same way as the Protestant ministers were in New England. So that's where I think it begins, the notion that God is an American. It begins in New England. And the degree to which the seventeenth- and eighteenth-century New England village is the primary source and model for our American social democracy and provides the template for representative government in America, the degree to which that form of democracy came to be practiced across all the thirteen colonies, is the degree to which God is central to American political thinking and American political and social discourse. It's the main mark of the ascendancy of the New England form of political comity.

Which brings us to the question of taxes. Why did the issue elicit such a strong response, such a violent reaction, in 1776? I don't think it was a simple matter of taxes per se. It was taxation without representation. That's how it was phrased. They weren't simply rebelling against taxes. They were rebelling against control from abroad by the English Parliament and Crown. By the late eighteenth century—the 1750s, '60s, '70s—New

Englanders had gotten used to representing themselves in their own towns, their own counties, their own colonies. They elected their own officials, passed their own regulations, and taxed themselves. In other words, they had already by then cut the umbilical cord between the mother country and the colonial child, and in this they were far ahead of the other colonies.

Remember, politically speaking, the American Revolution has its ideological and intellectual roots mainly in New England. But in economic terms, it finds its energy and roots in the South, in Virginia and Maryland and the Carolinas. There, to the landed gentry and the slave holders, given the size and scale and wealth of the plantation system in the South, it made economic sense to become a distinct nation independent of the mother country. As inevitably happens, when the wealth produced by a colony seems to be returning from the source to the mother country, the colonials feel cheated. To no small degree, they were right to feel cheated.

So again there was a mixed set of motives—more idealistic, ideological, and political motives in the North, and more commercial and economic in the South. But they served each other's needs. The North gave the South the ideological, intellectual, and political rationale for independence. The South gave the North the economic means and justification, and the belief that, should the colonies unite, they could survive independently without the mother country. That's why they pulled together. Simply, the South couldn't survive independence without the North; the North couldn't survive without the South. So these thirteen separate and disparate colonies managed to unite out of both practical and ideological reasons. From there they managed to pull off an extraordinary war of independence and successfully separate themselves from what was, at the time, the most powerful nation on earth.

Was our War of Independence a revolt or a revolution? I think it was a true revolution, because it articulated, for the first time and for all to use, the most radical concept of democracy then on the planet: the idea of representative government—governance obtained without a monarchy of any sort, without a nobility, without any rank of nobility; governance by and for the governed. Though it took a decade before the French managed to apply that radical concept to their own situation, it should be noted that the vocabulary and ideals for the American Revolution come straight out of the European Enlightenment. America's so-called founding fathers, Thomas Paine, Thomas Jefferson, Ben Franklin, James Madison, and so on, took their vocabulary from European Enlightenment thinking. They articulated it on the ground and institutionalized it in Philadelphia in 1776 and again in 1787 in our founding and guiding documents: the Declaration of Independence and the United States Constitution. It was a revolutionary concept at that time, a radical break with the European notion of comity and authority. Yes, it was to some degree, by today's standards, an elitist movement. Most successful political movements are. The ideas and the expression of those ideas came from the top down. And yes, only white men with property were qualified to vote. Several million slaves were excluded from this process. Women were excluded. And in the dispensation of proportional representation in Congress, each slave was to count as three-fifths of a person, which gave the South a numerical bulge sufficient to balance against the more populous North. So by definition it was elitist many times over. But at the same time it was established that there would be no nobility and no monarchy, giving life to what was essentially a populist notion. Imbedded in the words chosen carefully by those white men were concepts of freedom and inclusion that would in time carry weight and intentions far beyond anything the founding fathers may have intended. If we go back to that moment in time, to 1787 when the Constitution was ratified, we have to admit that those early Americans produced some very radical documents. We have to wait until a decade later, in France, to see anything as radical as that again. The French gave the Americans the vocabulary, the Americans created the institutions to express that vocabulary, and then the French took the institutions back a decade later. The Americans took the theory, made it pragmatic and applied it, and then the French brought the applications back home and, in a more rad-ical form, put them to use there—a cycle that's character-istic of both cultures, one we've seen over and over in many different fields of human endeavor. And today, two and a quarter centuries later, we are still waiting for the inspiring words in those radical documents to have their full effect.

AMERICANS HAVE tended to misread and understate how difficult and long was the war against the British army, because the Civil War, when it was over, quickly became a great distorting screen or scrim for us. When you read documents, including letters and so forth, written by Americans *before* the Civil War, where they're looking back towards the Revolution barely half a century earlier, Americans viewed the Revolutionary War with greater clarity of thought and with greater understanding of its costs and sacrifices, its duration and difficulty, than they did after the Civil War. The Civil War threw such a huge shadow across America and the American imag-ination that it was difficult, after the war, to look back and imagine what it must have been like to con-duct and finally win that Revolution, that seven-year war against the British.

Our War of Independence was fought by untrained soldiers, laymen, farmers, and mechanics, led by young men in their twenties and thirties, with very few supplies and arms, against the largest, best-trained, most professional army in the world. Through the tactical brilliance of George Washington and several others—and the support of the French, and the Marquis de Lafayette, and other Continental Europeans as well—they were able to prevail. It was extraordinary. And it was not at all inevitable or even likely. It wasn't something that you could have predicted at the time. And right up to the very end of the war it looked as though the Americans would not prevail.

Speaking of the Marquis de Lafayette, he lived a very long life, and in 1824, about ten years before he died, he returned to the United States for a triumphal tour to all the places he had been during the war, starting in New York and making his way to the South, the middle Atlantic states, north to Boston, and all the way up the Hudson River to Saratoga, where I live for much of the year. In each place he was greeted like a conquering hero. No foreigner at that time, and perhaps no foreigner since, has ever come to America and been received with such jubilation and excitement and vast crowds as when Lafayette returned. What that shows us is that a whole generation later he was still seen as a grand hero, a hero of the first order. That's how powerful the memory of the war and the image of Lafayette's role in it were in the American imagination in the years leading up to the Civil War. But if Lafayette had lived long enough to show up today in New York, or at any time after 1861, he wouldn't draw a very big crowd. Only a couple of curiosity seekers and history buffs would turn out to see him. He'd be disappointed. The role of Lafayette, and with it the memory and true meaning of the Revolutionary War, have diminished to the point where they are lost now, mostly forgotten, part of a past to which we're no longer connected.

The BLOODY MASSACRE per

BRITISH TROOPS
SHOOTING AT
CROWD IN BOSTON
MASSACRE, CA.
1770

in King—t—Street ... on March 5th 1770 by a party of the 29th. REGt.

BUTCHER'S HALL

Engrav'd Printed & Sold by PAUL REVERE BOSTON

THE POWER OF WORDS

R ALPH ELLISON, the great American novelist, refers to the Declaration of Independence and the Constitution as "our sacred documents," as if they were biblical, as if they were divinely ordained. And Americans generally do view the Constitution and the Declaration of Independence essentially as divinely ordained and sacred in some way. Perhaps it's because of the poetic, almost biblical language of the Declaration of Independence, and because of the institutions embodied in the Constitution. They sound more biblical than legalistic. Those two documents, more than any other writings, unite the elements at war in the American imagination and American culture, and in the divided American public—the warring elements being racial, cultural, economic, regional, and historic.

I spoke earlier about a few of these conflicts. It is only through the Declaration of Independence—the extraordinary brilliance of it, both the precision and the vagaries of it—and the beautiful, delicate balancing act that the Constitution lays out between the three branches of the government—the executive, the representative, and the judicial—that we're able to bring together these conflicting elements that lie at the heart of the American imagination and the American past. I think it's by means of an intuitive recognition of that fact that we Americans regard the documents as sacred. Even Ralph Ellison, a black novelist in the mid-twentieth century, a man who knew better than most how far we still have to go before they will be in full effect, could nonetheless refer to them as "our sacred documents," for they embodied the guiding principles of all Americans, his as much as mine.

It's fascinating to contrast the United States Constitution with the constitutions of our individual fifty states. Each state has its own constitution, usually a litany of laws. It's the same with most national constitutions—the new constitution of Iraq, or the French Constitution, for example. They're deliberately oriented to a specific people, place, and time. But the American Declaration of Independence has a poetic loftiness that universalizes its ambitions. It speaks of mankind as much as of Americans. And the institutions laid out in the American Constitution are so decorously balanced that it manages to universalize our country's political structure, too. Both of our founding documents really are extraordinary acts of creative genius.

⌐≈≈≈⌐

AMERICA WASN'T always nationalistic, consistently and purely, the way we have become in the late twentieth and early twenty-first centuries. There was the tumult of conflicting impulses, especially leading up to the Civil War, when roughly as many Americans wanted to break away from a unified national identity as wanted to extend that national identity. Southerners wanted to split off early on and go their own way, hoping to pull Cuba and the Caribbean into their sphere of influence. Northern New Englanders at different times wanted to join Canada. Texas set itself up as a separate nation in the 1840s, and California was briefly a separate nation.

It was really only after the Civil War that the United States became America the nation-state. There was a shift there in terminology, too, moving from being the United States of America to "America," from being a fairly loose consortium of separate but united states, pulled apart at times, pulling together at others, into something that was a single word: America. Which is a very different kind of creature than the United States. It's more nearly mythical and points a bony finger back to the European discovery of the continent, remaking that "discovery" in its image, no longer true to the facts of the matter in all their complexity. It was the Civil War that turned our flickering national identity into a sacred flame. And that was reinforced in the twentieth century when America became a player on the world stage, starting with the Spanish American War, as we call it, which involved the taking over of Cuba and the Philippines and expelling the Spanish from their sphere of influence in the Caribbean.

In the twentieth century, when America became a central player on the world stage, our national identity got another push, right through the century and up to the Cold War. Of course at the end of the Cold War, America emerged as the single dominant power in the West, however brief our star turn may be. By then our national impulses were running at full throttle. But we do well to remember that this was never all that we were. The separate impulses that have driven us drive us still. Keep in mind that we began fleeing and resisting empire, and our national identity didn't start out strong—in fact, it started very weak—so it may not be our true nature after all, and surely it is not permanent.

WITH THE rise of nationalism, of course, has come all the other forms of idiocy that reinforce the identification with, and worship of, the state. That danger always lies at the heart of nationalism. Racial purity, the notion of religious purity, cultural hegemony—these sick social needs emerge almost inevitably and everywhere from nationalism. W. H. Auden called nationalism a disease, and it is a disease. You can see it clearly in films, because the advent of the American film industry early in the twentieth century happens to coincide with the ascendance of nationalism in America. The first great American film is *The Birth of a Nation*, which equates the birth of our nation with the achievement of racial purity in the era of Reconstruction, the 1870s to the 1890s. The bloody, brutal work of the Ku Klux Klan is a horrific, shameful episode in our history, yet right there in our first cinematic self-portrait it's presented without apology. It's even made a point of pride. It cannot be ignored that *The Birth of a Nation* is an extraordinary film—one that's loathsome ethically, and that's politically and spiritually loathsome as well, and yet artistically it's great. It's like a Leni Riefenstahl Nazi propaganda film, yet it's also the fountainhead of what is perhaps the most extraordinary art form to be developed in the twentieth century.

So our words—the words of our founding documents—have had their work cut out for them. Not only must they stand against the disease of nationalism, and the dreams of glorious wealth through exploitation, they must also withstand the visual siren song of what has become our mythmaking industry in Hollywood and elsewhere, which has occasionally been subversive, but more often serves the pleasure of the powers that be.

Again and again in America today the beliefs of Christian fundamentalists—which are not only biblical but full-on apocalyptic, including as they do the nearness of the End Time and the Second Coming of Christ—are an increasingly large component of the American character. The fundamentalist vision, representing now a very wide swath of the American people, those who have not been embraced by any other orthodoxy, who live in "fly-over" country and are not the consumers or even the citizens that media mavens and opinion-makers in New York, Los Angeles, Washington, DC, and San Francisco like to think about, hearkens back to that inherent conflict I was speaking of earlier, between the institution of slavery and the promises of the Declaration of Independence and the Constitution, between the

Plantation and New Jerusalem. It took a civil war to resolve the conflict between the materialistic, racist reality of slavery and the essentially spiritual language of the Declaration of Independence and the Constitution, an inherent conflict that could only be resolved by means of the most costly war, in terms of human life, in our history. And it continued to be fought long after the war was over, through the years of Reconstruction, which *The Birth of a Nation* portrays, well into the twentieth century, all the way up to the 1960s and the civil rights movement. We— we white people—thought the conflict was resolved, in legal terms, and also in emotional and psychological terms. The promise fulfilled. But the truth is, it still hasn't been. The question of who can claim to bear our spiritual mantle as Americans still has not been answered.

The narrative of race

THERE IS an argument, generally coming from the Right, most persistently from the South, that the Civil War was fought over states' rights. And in a sense that's true. There was a central political issue, a constitutional issue, to be settled. But the states' right they were fighting for was the right to own slaves, the right to own other human beings. If it had been the right to tax themselves or raise their own militia or set aside public lands, no one would have gone to war over it. But it was the right to own slaves. So at the heart of it, the Civil War was a conflict about race, and that conflict lies at the heart of American history. Race is our great central story. Our ur-narrative. Everything returns to it, because in it is contained the larger question of where we stand in relation to our God and whether in the end we are moral animals or not. This is why a founding document that contains language that addresses this issue can be sacred in the same way to a black American and a white American.

The narrative of race began when the first Europeans arrived off the shores of the Caribbean islands and Florida, off the shores of Jamestown, Virginia, and off the shores of New England, where they met the dark-skinned people who happened to reside here already, people whom the Europeans chose to deal with in the majority of cases as less than human, treating them instead as human chattel, as being less worthy of natural respect and kind treatment than draft animals like horses or cattle. The rationale was twofold: first, that the economic usage or exploitation of them wouldn't have made sense unless they could be seen as lesser creatures, and second, because they were not Christians.

So from the very beginning, racial differentiation was situated at the hot center of the American imagination. And it's still there. It's still central. Our most terrible wars have been fought over it. Our most important political conflicts have been waged over it. Nearly every political campaign comes down to it, even today. Our economic lives are shaped by it. Our views of the rest of the world are determined by it. How we treated Southeast Asians in the latter part of the 1960s and early '70s, how we're dealing today with the Arab world, how we treat Africans—it all comes down to race in some fundamental way. I don't mean to sound overly reductive, but when you lift the rock of American society and you look under it, you almost always see race. It's at the dark heart of our conflicted nature. We are in a sense a schizophrenic people. I don't mean that we have a split identity, but we have a deeply conflicted, self-canceling identity. We're at war with ourselves. And this explains, I think, why we so often march off to war against others—as horrific as foreign wars are, they are much easier for us at home than it would be to face the internal battles of being at war within ourselves. Anything to avoid the war within ourselves that is still actively forging our identity, a war whose outcome hasn't been decided yet; and until it is, we won't really know who we are. That is what people mean, I think, when they say that we are still a young nation.

❦

THERE IS no American Revolutionary War work of fiction that everyone has read. And so our Revolutionary War isn't alive in the American imagination. Interestingly, there is an English book about the French Revolution that everyone's read or seen the movie adaptation of, and that's Charles Dickens's *A Tale of Two Cities*. Because of it, the French Revolution as a symbol of popular violence is very much alive in the American imagination. The vision of The Terror comes from England to the United States in the nineteenth century, and it sticks. It's a fearsome image to us. I don't think Americans really have any particular historically informed view of the French Revolution. We don't know very much about it, and most of us probably couldn't even date it. Nor do Americans have a visceral idea of our own revolution, of the suffering or the violence involved; instead it has been sugar-coated and cerebralized almost to the point where people think of it as nothing more than a great big roundtable discussion about freedom and representation, instead of the knock-down drag-out brawl of guerrilla warfare through shifting alliances and class conflict between rich and poor that it really was. And the closest thing we have to that sense of upheaval isn't our own revolution, but instead the French one, which thanks to Dickens has been represented to Americans imagistically by the movies and in literature. And it's an image that terrifies people who feel somewhat unstable to begin with. If you feel slightly unsure of what the proper role of citizens should be, and you see this vision of democracy unleashed—mob rule, terror, class war—then you react with fear. I really do blame it all on Dickens. If it were not for that novel and the film made of the novel, I don't think Americans would view the French Revolution any differently than the way that we do the Russian Revolution. And the Russian Revolution, even though it brought Communism into the world and was a hundred times more brutal, doesn't terrify us.

The Russian Revolution strikes us as merely fascinating, whereas the French version strikes us as threatening, and our very own revolution somehow doesn't strike us as fascinating *or* threatening. Quite the opposite. Boring and comforting. And I believe that in the vividness of the French Revolution to us, in the vividness and the emblematic power of it, you can see something that is very much alive today in America, though not much talked about, which is our fear of democracy taken to its extreme. We who are educated and opinionated and lead comfortable lives here in the US, where the quality of life for the middle class and the upper class provides, despite looming problems, opportunities for a secure, self-aggrandizing way of life, we fear the loss of social control that extreme democracy represents. We don't fear Communism, Leninism, or even Stalinism as much. The notion of an oppressive and restrictive totalitarian society doesn't have the same chilling vividness for us as the chaos of pure democracy, and that we associate with the French Revolution.

THE FIRST American immigrants, not counting the colonists, came over unwillingly: they were the enslaved Africans, who didn't come here out of any volition of their own. But they were still, after all, immigrants. And they were the first to arrive in large numbers from more or less the same region of the world, which happened to be West Africa, rather than Europe, so we have to count them and must remember that when we talk about waves of immigrants the Africans were the first. I think too often we don't want to consider them as such, and in denying them their identity as immigrants from someplace else, we assign to them the identity of slaves and the descendants of slaves. But slavery wasn't their identity, it was their circumstance. It was not who they were, but what was done to them.

After the Africans, huge numbers of immigrants from Europe started to arrive in the middle of the nineteenth century, first a great many thousands from Germany, but then mostly immigrants from northwest Europe—white Protestant Christians who were relatively easily assimilated, even if they weren't middle class. And then came the Irish, who were mostly poor and Catholic, coming to a Protestant country, as it was then, a literate country, and they were for the most part illiterate. They arrived in great numbers in the 1840s in flight from extreme poverty, just seeking the fundamentals—food, shelter, clothing—seeking little more than a chance to survive and, if they were lucky and plucky, to thrive. And that became more or less the pattern for a long period of time, seventy-five or more years. The Chinese arrived from Asia in as great a number as the Irish. Then came the Eastern Europeans, the Jews, the Poles, Italians, Greeks, and so on.

In each case they brought with them their own cultural norms from their country of origin, which they then tried to integrate with the norms of the Americans already in residence here, with greater or lesser degrees of success. It was more difficult when the immigrants' religious practices were different—Catholic instead of Protestant; Buddhist, Muslim, Confucian, or Hindu instead of Christian—or when the immigrants were seen as racially different.

There is an interesting book called *How the Irish Became White* by the historian Noel Ignatiev. It describes the parallels between the essentially racist early portrayals of the Irish in American newspapers, in American writing and in early films—as a sexually reckless, self-indulgent, musically inclined, happy-go-lucky people—and the way that African Americans were portrayed in the same period, and even until recently. The same kinds of stereotypes and prejudices were applied to both groups.

When I was growing up in the 1940s and '50s, my father and other Anglo-American men of his generation used to refer to Italians as "Guineas." I never knew what a Guinea was until I was an adult and saw that it was a nineteenth-century word for Africa, and thus for Africans. What that means to me is that as recently as the 1950s, Italians and other Mediterraneans were seen as racially different from us white folks. Even as a kid I thought this was very weird. But we Americans use racial stereotypes in order to talk about anyone who is different in any way—culturally different, religiously different, linguistically different. It doesn't matter. We'll find a way to enshrine the difference in racial terms.

This goes back to what I was saying earlier about the obsession with race in the American imagination. Each wave of immigrants has had to deal with this American obsession. Even when they were white, they had to deal somehow with the ancient and profound racial anxiety that lies at the center of the American psyche. Jews coming from Eastern Europe certainly felt it. Greeks felt it, Italians felt it, and today Hispanics feel it. Black Americans felt it for the longest time and may have the deepest understanding of it. Our racial anxiety could be amusing, it's so ridiculous, if the way it has been inflicted on people weren't so horribly cruel and brutal.

Reel Three

CONQUEST OF
THE IMAGINATION

MOST IMMIGRANTS who arrived in the USA had no intention of going home. Only the Cubans have thought of going home in some imaginary post-Castro era, as if that one man were a historical aberration, rather than part of that country's long march towards revolution, and his death will return their country to some pre-revolutionary state. But when other immigrants came to America, not only did they invent a new life, moving in powerful, irreversible ways to start life over, they also ended their old lives. They cut themselves off from old languages, cultural associations, ethnic and religious ties, and created new ones. It's very important to understand this process if we're going to grasp how the US was able, over the last 150 years or so, to absorb wave after wave of very different kinds of people. It didn't matter whether they came from Korea, India, South America, Greece, Africa, Poland, or Ireland—that same process operated. A new identity was embraced, an old identity was discarded. The interesting exception, as I said, has been the Cubans, who put themselves in a holding pattern. In their minds, when Castro dies they'll return home. Consequently, they haven't assimilated. Mexicans in Manchester, New Hampshire; Nicaraguans in Portland, Oregon; Vietnamese in Houston, Texas, have been assimilated; but Cubans in Miami have not. They've kept their bags packed.

In Europe over the last twenty-five to forty years, the migrations have mostly been from Islamic countries, and Europeans are dealing not so much with immigrants, as with migrants who have a dream of going back and who, like the Cubans, strive to maintain the ties and cultural connections to the mother nations, their places of origin. And that has made it much more difficult to embrace the newcomers, as we have seen over recent years particularly.

I can't say exactly why it's been so difficult in Europe otherwise, except to say that this may not be exceptional. It may be the rule. And it may be that the American example, as it has stood for the last one and three-quarters centuries, may be the exception. For the fact is that when people come to the US they are coming to a place where the mythology of starting over is so powerful as to be, paradoxically, the very essence of what it means to be American. Throughout most of our history this has been the draw. You didn't just come here to make money to send home until you yourself could return. America was not simply a place to find employment; it was a place to start your life over. It goes back to that very early version of the American Dream that we were trying to describe. Central to the original American Dream is the idea of starting over. It was economic, too, yes. You could improve your financial life and your lot in life. And it was also a virtuous place. You could live free and with dignity, certainly. That too was part of the myth. But along with those material and spiritual aspects there was also the central myth of starting your life anew, of being a child again—remember the Fountain of Youth. That's a very powerful lure. And it worked. It really does work. Because if you're going to start over, you have to kill the past, and Americans are great at killing the past.

LOOKING AGAIN at books, at literature—because I feel the books that last open a window into the soul of our people—so many of our favorite novels and films are about acquiring a new identity, about changing one's life. Go west, young man or woman! Go south! Light out for the territory! Hit the road, Jack. Change your identity, reject your past, and become a new person. Not necessarily a powerful person, although that's always a possibility in America, but a new person. The novels and the films of the open road are all about that. It's a kind of film and novel that's specific to America— getting in a car and going west, or getting in a covered wagon and going west, or getting on a raft and going down the river, and changing as a result, becoming a different person.

The two most powerful American novels from the nineteenth century are Herman Melville's *Moby Dick* and Mark Twain's *Adventures of Huckleberry Finn*, and they both involve a transformation, a spiritual transformation. One is a search starting in New England that leads across the Western oceans on a quest to kill a great white whale. The other is a search by a white boy and a black man for racial clarity on a raft floating down the Mississippi River. *Moby Dick* is a story of an obsessed, monomaniacal white man in charge of a racially mixed crew, and race is a big factor in its unfolding. There's a kind of intimacy between the races that's pointed to and celebrated in the novel, and in the film, too, a story about following a possibly mad captain into the Western sea in search of a white whale—a total abstraction, an absolute truth, a religious truth, let's say. These vivid adventure tales describe rites of passage through hundreds or thousands of miles of travel and across the great psychological expanse of the racial divide that have been central aspects of the American experience from the very beginning.

It is intriguing to consider how the American conquest of the West differed from the Europeans' colonization in Africa and elsewhere during the nineteenth century. There are obvious similarities, and there are interesting differences. The West, to Americans in the East, right from the very beginning, only seemed an extension of the East. It was not a different continent that belonged to someone else and that needed to be conquered somehow. Going out and taking control of the West and settling it was our "Manifest Destiny." It was a way, perhaps the only one available at the time, to live out our destiny as Americans. And the West was ours from the start. It wasn't just a place in the imagination, an *ultima thule* at the far end of the world. You can see it in the very first colonial maps, where they extend the states of Connecticut and Virginia and various other states deep into the continent—when they didn't even know what was out there. It was made legal and binding with the Louisiana Purchase from France in 1803, when Americans acquired ownership of the enormous tract of the West, and President Jefferson sent Lewis and Clark to make their exploratory passage through it, to report back to Washington what, in fact, we had actually purchased. So it's not the same thing as the

English, and the French, and other Europeans out looking for the source of the Nile or the Congo and seizing control of the continent from the Africans in order to establish colonies. Americans felt they were exploring their own backyard. Never mind the fact that there happened to be all these native people—hundreds of thousands of them, maybe even millions, living in societies that were in some ways just as civilized and in some ways more civilized than European societies— living across that vast tract that Americans regarded as their own backyard, the backyard of New York and the backyard of Virginia. So when Americans moved west they weren't colonizing; they were simply making themselves at home. It involved a very different mentality. And they were dislodging the people that lived there as if *they* were the invaders. The native people were not regarded as the owners and caretakers of this vast piece of real estate. They were seen as trespassers on our property. In some ways, though, our colonizing history runs parallel to the European colonization of Africa with a vengeance; it starts with the Spanish American War, conquering the Philippines, colonizing Cuba and parts of Asia, and colonizing parts of Central and South America and the Caribbean. Thanks to our nineteenth-century takeover of the West, our colonial ambitions got slightly postponed, and unlike the Europeans' colonial ambitions, didn't begin to be realized until just prior to the beginning of the twentieth century.

Still, our earlier conquest of the western half of North America, factually and economically, bore an astounding resemblance to European colonization of Africa and elsewhere. But not in how we viewed it or represented it to ourselves. In a way, the Western movie genre makes that point. In the movies it's never a story of colonization. It's a story of taking what is legitimately destined to be your own and establishing governance and residence in it. The first thing you have to do is clear these blasted Indians out of it. The next thing you have to do is build a fort so that you can establish a military base for the protection of the citizenry from the Indians who are left. And then you put up a log cabin and a fence, and you put cattle and sheep inside the fence, and you plow the fields and plant corn and wheat. So there's this gradual domestication or taming of the wilderness. That's the operation that's going on in the American imagination. And of course what these films do, what all films do, is dramatize and reinforce what's already in the viewers' imagination.

In our collective imagination, the Indians are seen as part of the untamed wilderness and have to be expunged in some way. Then you're free to cut down the forest and use the logs to build the fort. That way you'll have cleared a field or two, where you can build a house and raise domestic animals. You can almost see the whole mythologized history of civilization unfolding in a typical Western movie. We went from being hunter-gatherers to farmers to villagers. And then we built cities. It's a fascinating genre if you look at it that way. That is how I think Americans view the move West. We were taming our own wilderness, domesticating it, making it fit for the American nuclear family. Which of course is always white, middle class, with 2.4 children.

To Americans, this vivid and powerful sequence of images somehow goes to the heart of the American Dream. You can go west. You can find land and build a home. You can establish a free and democratic, supportive community, and you can start your life over. One of the things that is true in all those classic Western movies is that there's very little reference to where the settlers came *from*, whether they came from Boston, Philadelphia, or Atlanta. They don't refer back; they're always going forward. The Western movie embodies the American Dream in very significant ways. And the forces which obstruct or deflect the American Dream from its realization in the Western are often presented in racial terms, as Indians or Mexicans, manifestations of the Other. They're not the forces of civilization, as we say. So usually the plot unfolds from the point where the savage or the non-Christian or the non-white Other is making it difficult for us to establish domestic bliss as ordained in the US Constitution, the Declaration of Independence, and maybe the Bible, too.

Ultimately—and it gets tricky here—the path to the American Dream has become a tortured path. It has led to our building an empire. The small engine of one person's dream of starting over has somehow morphed into the mighty engine of Manifest Destiny, of empire. From that point of view, it may be a psychotic dream, no less powerful for that—more powerful, rather, but unhealthy, an expression of dysfunction and disease. It is psychotic, in a way, to think that you can start your life over, that there's no such thing as the past. It's a kind of madness to think that you can always improve your life, financially, economically, generation after generation, with each generation succeeding further, and not recognize that this is simply an impossibility, one that ultimately, inevitably, like any Ponzi scheme, will lead to failure. And the economic demands and expectations that back this distorted dream are always going to be in conflict with the ideals of democracy. They demand and expect one person to trample on another. This conflicts with the democratic ideals in our sacred documents and in our hearts.

The great wide open spaces where we raised cows and sheep and grew vast fields of corn, rye, and wheat provided a kind of motor to drive the empire. But then the industrial might of the cities—midwestern cities like Chicago, and Detroit, and Cleveland—became the motor that set the wheels of empire turning. You had to find consumers for all this. And that required another kind of empire, a more mundane one based on the European system: simply the exploitation of other people's raw materials and labor. As a result, starting in the late nineteenth century, in Central America in particular and in South America, later in Asia and Africa and then in the Middle East, Americans got very deeply involved in gathering, controlling, and exploiting raw material and labor in other parts of the world. It was the traditional European model for empire, the new and improved version. More recently, with the increasing globalization of the economy, American corporations and successive administrations of both parties have worked very hard to ensure that we are at the center of the world economy, controlling as much of the raw processes as possible, more than any other single country in the world, with the possible exception of China, so that now the US is situated at the center of the globalization tsunami. We're doing it in a way that's familiar to us, as the continuation of the impulses we acted on in the late nineteenth century in the movement west, as if it all already belonged to us through Manifest Destiny, as if the whole world now were our backyard, and as if others who might be there already were trespassers.

There's the old American story of the three generations, one that goes back all the way to the American Revolution, to John Adams, a founding father and president. In the story the first generation is a laborer so that the second generation can go to college and become a professional person so that the third generation can live a life of leisure, or maybe become an artist.

So the first generation basically sacrifices itself for the benefit of the second, and the second generation in turn sacrifices itself for the benefit of the third. All done willingly, because the belief in progress goes very deep, the belief that the sacrifice will reap a bountiful reward, a willingness to give up one's life that I don't think is as deeply imbedded in the European imagination. And you still see it today. You see wave after wave of people from Mexico and the Caribbean, from Africa, Asia, Central and South America, who are willing to work very hard for a lifetime at menial jobs in order that their children can get an education so that they don't have to do menial work, they can become lawyers and doctors and professional people, so that the third generation can go to university and study the fine arts, the humanities, philosophy, and so forth.

I taught at Princeton University for many years, and it was always the case. I taught the ambitious children of Indians, Koreans, Jamaicans, and so on. The parents had sacrificed and sometimes humiliated themselves working at menial jobs so that these children could go to university, and they were all studying medicine, law, business, those sorts of professions. And you know that their children in turn, when they go to university, will study music and art, philosophy, the humanities. That succession, that commitment to change over the course of several generations, provides a lot of energy, a lot of momentum, a lot of labor and life-long personal sacrifice for at least two and sometimes three or more generations.

The people who changed the world in the early twentieth century were not the Rockefellers and the Carnegies and the Fords. It was the people who worked for them who changed the world. The workers provided industry with the power. The half-dozen people at the top who made the great fortunes—the Fords and the Rockefellers, the Astors and the Carnegies—they didn't provide American industry with its strength. It was the millions of Americans who worked on the assembly lines, in the mines, in the fields, in the shipping yards, on the docks and the railroads, and so on. They were the ones who changed the world. That's why I'm still talking about the American Dream. Because there is an ongoing battle for the right to restore that dream or see it replaced by the dream of empire.

Rockefeller didn't believe in the American Dream, but everyone who worked for him did. He believed in the dream of empire. Ford didn't believe in the American Dream, but all those guys assembling Model Ts and Model As down on the assembly line, they did. Those Irishmen and those Italians and those Greeks, they did. All those Hungarians and Poles in the steel yards in Pittsburgh working for Carnegie, they're the ones who changed American society. Carnegie didn't. They sacrificed and worked very, very hard for many, many years. For generations. And the dream they believed in was still believable, because it was human-scale, focused on individuals, and strengthened through family ties and in local communities and labor unions. It wasn't the distorted and corrupted dream of Empire.

So of course my American heroes are not the Carnegies and the Fords. They're the people in the mines and on the assembly lines, in the steelyards and on the docks. They're the people who laid the railroads across this country, the Chinese, and the Irish who were digging the canals. Every society has its captains of industry. Europe had its captains of industry in the first two decades of the twentieth century. What Europe didn't have was that enormous labor pool willing to sacrifice itself in the workplace, a labor pool that was for the most part literate—that's important as well—who forged our national identity as a nation of immigrants, with not one but many identities, who came together to sacrifice and to build.

THE GRAPES OF
WRATH, 1940

OF MAN AND MACHINES

A MERICANS HAVE always believed in the almost spiritual beauty of machinery. Our early heroes are people like Benjamin Franklin. If we put Ben Franklin on the same pedestal as we do George Washington, James Madison, and Thomas Jefferson, it's not because of his statesmanship, although Franklin was in fact a great statesman. No, we honor him because he was a classic American tinkerer, a true mechanic in the most basic sense. And better yet, a self-taught American mechanic.

Other American tinkerer heroes include the Wright brothers, Robert Fulton and his steamboat, Thomas

Edison, and of course Henry Ford. But the Henry Ford we admire is not the international industrialist; it's the young mechanic in the back of a Detroit garage putting together the first Model T by himself. We like to think of ourselves as a country of mechanics, self-taught, by and large. So, yes, we do idealize technology, but the object of our worship isn't the wizardry and magic of technology, but almost the very opposite. Americans have a home-spun and down-to-earth curiosity about the ways of the physical world and the mechanics of nature and a com-plementary belief that they can be known and controlled.

American likes and dislikes, which are after all important clues to our identity, were never incidental or coincidental. We're very pragmatic and materialistic as a culture. Consequently, we admire mechanics—not abstract scientists or intellectuals, but applied scien-tists and the writers of adventure stories about whaling ships and runaways on a raft. And we have been that way from the very beginning. You can go back to the six-teenth and the seventeenth centuries in American his-tory and see how the first settlers were cut off from the European sources of early industrial production. They were in the wilderness, or on the edge of the wilderness, in Virginia, in New England, in New York. They had to make do with what they had, and they didn't have much. They had to cut down the trees; they had to build bricks from the riverbank clay; they had to work with what was literally at hand. So there developed a tremendous affection and respect for the mechanic and the handmade machine. This was how we conquered possibly our fiercest adversary, the wilderness, not the mythical one but the real wilderness of seventeenth- and eighteenth- and even nineteenth-century America, vast and unbroken, spanning nearly every possible extreme of climate, weather, and geography.

By the time our handmade machines have evolved into assembly lines, by the time we have access to highly technological industry, we've got a jump on the rest of the world because we've brought with us a profound affection for both the mechanic—we like and admire Bill Gates and Steve Jobs more than the billionaires who made theirs speculating with other peoples' money—and for the technology the mechanic creates and utilizes. We're not superstitious about it the way some cultures are. We don't look down at physical work. And we don't look down at the mechanic or the engineer. We admire them. In a way, that admiration, genuine and heartfelt, has given us an advantage in the industrial and post-industrial eras.

In the 1930s, with the development of economic liberalism and a number of specific very important social modifications, there was a cascade of significant changes in American society, along with a concomitant change in certain traditional values. They occurred because of the Depression and our collective response as a society to that crisis. They occurred because of the failure of the great industrial fortunes to provide a social network that could endure a breakdown in the capitalist economic system. As a result of extreme widespread poverty, rather than the accumulation of wealth by a small segment of society, there occurred a change in traditional social values and a rise in liberal values and the belief that government had a responsibility to care for the welfare of its citizens.

Up to this point, until Franklin Roosevelt, until 1932, the idea that there must be a social net, administered by the federal government, by which the society as a whole looked after its weakest members, or to put it more exactly, looked after weak and strong equally, wasn't operational in American society. The New Deal and the establishment of certain institutions, like Social Security and so many other protective agencies that still function today, were created and came almost at once to seem natural and permanent. But at bottom what really took place first was a shift in our view of government's responsibility to the people. It was poverty, the poverty of the Depression, and the collapse of the capitalist economy that challenged those traditional nineteenth-century American assumptions and values and changed them—permanently, we thought.

Look at a film like *The Grapes of Wrath*. It portrays that period, the terrible poverty of that period, with enormous sympathy. It focuses on the little man, saying that he is an important person—this person who's lost his land, who's lost everything and is drifting west. He's impoverished and bitter; he doesn't have a home. And he's presented with great sympathy. You wouldn't see a movie like that in the 1920s. You wouldn't see the poor portrayed that way, not even by Chaplin. You don't see it until after the Depression, when core social values have shifted. In the 1940s you can look back at the Depression and the poor of that period who suffered so terribly, in the Dust Bowl and so on, in an extremely sympathetic way.

In the 1980s, during the presidency of Ronald Reagan, democracy and capitalism got married. This is something I remember clearly. They were no longer just compatible, they were seen to be the same, a single blended unit, inseparable. It was called Free Market Democracy. Of course now it's become the official guiding ideology of America, and it is spoken of as if it were always the case, as if it's written into the Declaration of Independence and the United States Constitution. But the first time we heard it articulated and expressed as a virtue was by Ronald Reagan in the 1980s, and then it became the new American ideal. Now it's how we justify conquest, how we justify economic exploitation, how we justify invasion and occupation. In his claims, it already existed as a main element of American political and economic ideology in the 1920s and even before. You see it in the era of the first Roosevelt, Theodore, at the turn of the century, where he claims to simultaneously export capitalism and democracy to the Philippines. As if the one provided a home for the other. It goes back even further than that. In the 1820s Americans created the country of Liberia in Africa. From the creators' point of view it was going to solve the problem of race in America because they were going to be able to send the Africans back to Africa. But the founders of Liberia also thought they were making Africa safe for the three Cs: Christianity, Capitalism, and Civilization. And today the same monstrous fantasy conjoining faith, profit, and progress into a holy alliance lies behind the melding of Capitalism and democracy for export. We're making Iraq safe for the three Cs: Christianity, Capitalism, and Civilization. Woodrow Wilson thought that if you took one, you got the other, a two-for-one deal. When you got Capitalism you got democracy. The bonus was that you also got Christianity and Civilization. It's a fantasy, a self-serving fantasy, of course. And it's also pure hucksterism, pure salesmanship, like the selling of dubious remedies from the back of a wagon. America has always been the home of hucksterism and extreme salesmanship.

Speeches made by George W. Bush in his first presidential election campaign and certain speeches made by others in the Republican Party at the time were anti-Wilsonian in spirit and intent. The Republicans presented themselves as noninterventionists, if not downright isolationists. But now, in the second Bush administration, they've come to justify their policies in very much the same way Woodrow Wilson did, with a belligerent foreign policy that is highly interventionist and brash, one which even many Republicans, members of the president's own party, are highly uncomfortable with and in some cases openly against.

The two earliest justifications for the European presence in North America were materialism and idealism. And the marriage of capitalism and democracy is a way to bring those two conflicting impulses together and ignore their inherent contradictions. The first version of the United States Constitution, before it was amended to eliminate slavery, demonstrated the same failed struggle to resolve the conflict between those two ideas. Abraham Lincoln said it, that there was in our Constitution an inherent contradiction between the ideals of democracy and the institution of slavery. Slavery meant submission to an economic and materialistic view; democracy articulated an idealistic one. When you marry capitalism and democracy you are trying to avoid that contradiction.

Politicians shift their rhetoric in order to suit their needs. They have always done that. So how did America in recent years shift from a tentative kind of isolationism to full-blown interventionism? You can see the former in the Bill Clinton years, in his reluctance to get involved in the Balkans, for example, ignoring the crisis in Rwanda and elsewhere. And in George W. Bush's campaign against Al Gore in 2000, Bush advertised himself as the presidential candidate who was not involved in nation-building and regime change and all that. His rhetoric was even more isolationist than his father's or Clinton's. But Bush wasn't the only one. We have over time swung back and forth between an isolationist impulse and an interventionist impulse. It has depended on our perceived economic needs, even though both isolationism and interventionism have always been justified and rationalized in idealistic terms. We justified intervention in Cuba and the Philippines in 1901, '02, and '03 in idealistic terms, when in fact we were playing catch-up with the European empire-builders. We justified staying out of World War I in isolationist terms because we weren't threatened militarily. But when our transport of goods to Europe was being threatened by German attacks on American shipping, we came into the war. It was economic, but we typically used the rationalization that we were rushing to the fight to save Europe. Nonsense. We were rushing to save American shipping. Why did America intervene so late? It simply wasn't in our economic interest to intervene before then. Foreign policy in the US, despite the rhetoric, has historically been driven by economics. It's always been the case. Because we are such a nationalistic people we're free to look on our relations with other countries in pragmatic and self-serving terms. Because we have a hierarchy of values that is based on nationalist priorities, we see our values and our needs as more important than those of anyone else on this planet. Nationalism gives you that right. Nationalism breeds exceptional-ism. So whatever happens to the Europeans or to any-one else on this planet is not as important as what happens to us. And when we say that we are exporting democracy and doing it in order to save the world, it sounds lovely. It's probably the only way you can get the American people to go to war, to sacrifice themselves. But in fact we go to war for our perceived economic needs. It's historically the case. Our isolation is phys-ical to begin with, and it has allowed us until recently to feel as though we were not threatened militarily by another country. We're not threatened by invasion from Canada or Mexico. And the seas have also pro-tected us, until very recently. Because of that physical isolation, our sense of ourselves in relation to the rest of the world has been one of fearlessness—that is to say, we had no fear of being invaded. If you're going to con-vince Americans to march off to war, you've got to make them feel they're threatened with imminent invasion. Witness the response to the attacks of 9/11. Bush and company got Americans to go to war by mak-ing us feel threatened.

In the early years of World War I, because of the attacks on our ships by German submarines, we were losing our ability to ship sold goods to Europe and to buy goods from Europe. The only thing that would sway the Congress and the Senate into declaring war was the belief that the American economy was under threat—that they couldn't ship cotton from the southern states or all those munitions that they manufactured in the factories of the North.

You can profiteer in wartime. People always make a lot of money in a war making and selling all those uniforms, tanks, weapons, bandages. There's a tremendous market for the products that get consumed in wars. So it was not to save Europe. It was surely not to save France from the Germans. Americans loved Germans in the early twentieth century.

So why does George W. Bush run America's foreign policy counter to the Republican Party's political ideology of the past fifty years? Because he has to. Bush has to resort to that kind of rhetoric in order to justify American sacrifices. Otherwise he couldn't get the American people to go on the march. He's tapping into that idealistic, religious, and nationalistic sense of self-importance, invoking it for his own reasons, of course. We've really gone back to the Eisenhower era, to the pre-containment years of the early Cold War. In talking about the call of history, Bush is trying to sound like Franklin Roosevelt in 1942. Because he's desperate. He's reaching for that particular brand of rhetoric because there is no other way to get the American people to make the sacrifices they have to make, no other way to get them to accept the brutal atrocities that we have committed, in this war in Iraq and elsewhere, and to throw overboard the essential rights that were promised to us, and by extension to everyone, in those sacred documents. We have to be made to feel that there's a cause worthy of those sacrifices, and so what Bush has been trying to do is instill in us that feeling for the cause, to make us feel that we're riding out on a white horse to save the world. We're making the world safe for those three Cs: Christianity, Capitalism, Civilization. He uses code to refer to Christianity, uses "free market" to refer to Capitalism, but feels comfortable invoking the word Civilization at will.

Meanwhile, the cause he is invoking simply isn't there. To embrace his ideology we must learn how to completely ignore the facts of our involvement in Iraq and to show an almost absolute disregard for the priorities of other peoples or other countries in the world. And yet, whenever other politicians or the Democrats or some in the media have attempted to call the President on the carpet, and to point out his utter disregard for the underlying facts, so far it hasn't seemed to stick. He isn't being impeached. His popularity is down, yes. But he seems to have brought the country down with him.

Woodrow Wilson had much the same problem that Bush has. His response was expressed a little more coherently and was perhaps a little more intellectually sophisticated than Bush & Co.'s. Wilson was, after all, a man of some education and a higher degree of literacy than Bush, perhaps. But essentially it came down to the same thing. It's been expressed differently over the years.

We mustn't forget that John F. Kennedy was responsible for the beginnings of the Vietnam War. It happened under his watch. He was a supposedly liberal Democratic president, but nonetheless he used the same rationale that Bush uses as he goes marching on today in Iraq. Wilson and Kennedy were more eloquently expressive than Bush, to be sure, but the same message was there. The underlying ideology was basically the same.

Do I think that our leaders are that cynical? Yes, I do, frankly. I think, however, that they have a system of beliefs such that they are convinced that this war is for the universal good; it is universally good to do whatever will benefit them and their friends. Reagan used that great phrase, "trickle-down economics." It was believed, and still is among Republicans, that if you gave tax cuts to rich people, eventually these benefits will trickle down to the poor, and the poor will be enriched from the rich people's having enjoyed a tax cut. A wonderful fantasy. It sounded too good to be true, and it was. We're still waiting for some of the enormous wealth that was generated by this subsidy to the richest Americans to trickle down. Of course it never did, so they gave another tax cut to the rich. The rich said, Don't worry, it's trickle-down economics; it's going to come down to you. They actually believed that. The rich believe that what's good for them is good for everybody.

I've spent hours talking to retired CIA agents who were involved in some of the worst atrocities—assassination of people like Patrice Lumumba, insurrections, coups, regime changes in places like Greece, and so on, around the world. Horrible things. And when they think you're part of the club, these old guys will sit there and talk about it fairly openly, because they think it was for the good of everybody. It was good for everybody that we went in there and knocked off Lumumba, because if we hadn't we would have had a Communist regime there. If we had a Communist regime in that central, very rich region of Africa, then the Communists would have had a foothold in Africa and da-da-da-da-da. It's a long, very old and tired story. We had to kill the Diems in Vietnam, too. It was good for everybody. The list of the leaders we have killed for the good of everybody isn't a short list, and of course the world is not a better place because of those assassinations. The world and our role in it is far worse because of them.

There was a film made a couple of years ago of the Graham Greene novel about Americans in Vietnam, *The Quiet American.* It's a beautiful portrayal of American self-serving innocence. Not quite cynicism, willful naiveté, usefully self-serving naiveté. And I think that's what this class of American politicians, captains of industry and so forth, have, a self-serving, useful naiveté. It allows them to rule conscience-free. It allows them to invite the poor, the blacks, the Hispanics, and so on, to sacrifice their children and to pay for the whole operation. The rich are not paying for this war. The poor are paying for this war, one way or another, and dying in it.

HANGING OF
CAPTAIN WIRZ,
1865

A VERY PECULIAR INSTITUTION

THE PRESIDENCY of the United States is a very peculiar institution. It's not a person, but a persona or "role" that a person fills or plays. And our president, in some ways even more than a monarch, represents in some very personal way the imagination and the mythology of the people who have elected him. We choose presidents, but we do not choose them on the basis of their experience or even their political views. We choose them based on how well they tap into our basic beliefs, how expressive they are of our own deepest national mythologies.

Woodrow Wilson, John F. Kennedy, Richard Nixon, Jimmy Carter, Ronald Reagan, Bill Clinton, and both George Bushes on some level all share this characteristic—they tap into and express back to us our deepest American mythologies. And mythologies are not necessarily highly intellectual or highly intelligent. They are basic, primal almost. You can tap into them from any point along the spectrum of education or intelligence. The presidency is the only seat of government where power resides in one person, and it is also a symbol of American personhood and American power. Both real and abstract, both factual and symbolic. And George W. Bush wouldn't have been elected if he hadn't managed to convince enough people—not a majority, as we know, but enough people, in enough places in the United States—that he was the exponent of their deepest, communal desires.

The same thing was true for Wilson, so we should not be surprised when he and Bush sound alike, even though one says it more eloquently than the other. The same thing with Kennedy. We should not be surprised when some justification Bush offers up reminds us suddenly of something Wilson or Kennedy said. Kennedy justified, for instance, the foiled invasion of Cuba. He condemned the Bay of Pigs invasion of Cuba only on pragmatic grounds; the invading force had not been well enough prepared. And he explained away the assassination of the

Diems in Vietnam and the beginning of the build-up of American forces in Vietnam.

I mean, this was John F. Kennedy, supposedly our most enlightened president of modern times. But we shouldn't be surprised when one president ends up sounding an awful lot like another president, even one with a very different level of education and native intelligence and so forth, because they were both chosen by the American people for the reason that they seemed to be the living embodiment of our deepest ideals and desires, no matter how contradictory those ideals and desires were.

No president or prime minister or monarch has quite the same role as the American president. He's part pope, part chief executive, and part monarch, and yet he's not any one of those things alone. There is a projection of religious or spiritual beliefs onto the president, a projection of belief in the president's possessing inherited, divinely endowed powers, like those of a monarch. But there is also trust and belief in the president as a pragmatic chief executive who gets things done. All these requirements are placed in our one and only president. Other countries divide them up. They have a king, and then they have prime ministers. Or they have a president and a prime minister, as they do in France. They divide the symbolic roles from the executive. From the beginning, we Americans have blended them. I think that goes back to our Revolutionary War, when there were very few models for parliamentary democracy around, and the temptation, which was very strong, was for us to replace one King George with the other King George, George Washington. Washington had to forcefully say, "I will not be your king." So, okay, we'll make you a president who has an extreme amount of power.

We provided Washington with a long term, four years. And until after Franklin Roosevelt, when the Constitution was amended to limit the office to two terms, those four years could legally be extended to twelve, sixteen, twenty. We left open the possibility of a monarch-like president. The role of the presidency was created to be an extraordinary role. And in a time of empire the president has the capacity to become imperial, to become an emperor. You see this happening now in the conflict between Congress and President Bush over his enthusiasm for suspending the rights of privacy and so forth, his insistence on acting in a unilateral way. We have become an empire, and in an empire the president moves in the direction of becoming an emperor. It's frightening! This may be the dark view of American history, but it is the view of history that is being promoted by the very people I'm talking about, those who wield power in our world today.

Homeland

LOOK AT how the map of the world changed after World War II. The powers that be in America felt it was in their interest to establish a balance of power in order to keep any single European nation from dominating Europe after the war. One way to do that would be to make sure it was possible for Germany to check France and also England. The Americans were playing the old balance-of-power game, making a series of realistic political moves to achieve that balance.

Despite Lafayette, our historical relationship with France was never the sibling relationship that our relationship with Germany was. And is. Culturally, Germany was a Protestant country and, especially in the early part of the twentieth century, the United States thought of itself as a Protestant country. Germany was a northern European country, and the United States at that time thought of itself as a northern country. So there was what I can only call a sibling affection between Germany and the US in the early twentieth century that lasted right up to the American involvement in World War II, up to 1941 really, before which we were not willing to see Germany's threat clearly.

And then right after the war ended the old relationship was renewed. It's interesting, the difference between the way America treated Japan after the war and the way we treated Germany, with the Marshall Plan for instance, allowing Germany essentially to re-arm, whereas that was forbidden to the Japanese. There was a different kind of control exerted over Japan after the war than over Germany. I think that was because there was a persistent identification with Germany, one that was much stronger than our identification with Japan, certainly, or even with France. It is interesting that whose side we were on wasn't the determining factor. Racial differences, or what were perceived to be racial differences, were certainly factors in the case of the Japanese. And the cultural resonance we felt with Germany, as well as certain geopolitical considerations, and other more psychological ones.

In the American mythology of Europe, France is seen as feminine and Germany as masculine, and Americans see their own country as masculine. There is a kind of male bonding with Germany. The French speak of the "mother country," and Germans speak of the "fatherland." Americans use neither and refer instead to the United States as our "homeland." What's interesting is just how distinct each of those three is, how different the nuance. So after the war, both mythology and realpolitik brought us back to our old closeness with Germany, which probably wasn't what anyone would have predicted, considering how recently we had been sworn enemies.

Acting on a world stage

ACTING ON the world stage in a spirit of partnership is a perennial problem for the United States. Accepting membership, parity, or equality with other countries in any international organization, for example, is something we have always found to be enormously difficult. Partly it's because of our unbridled nationalism and the belief that there are no higher priorities than our priorities; partly. it's the historical feeling of being distinct and separate from Europe and other parts of the world and seeing their quarrels as parochial, so not wanting to become dragged into them or involved in them in any way. There is that sense of our being special and distinct on the one hand, and not wanting to become embroiled in quarrels that are seen as belonging exclusively to Europeans, Africans, or Asians on the other.

But most importantly I think it's a refusal to allow what we regard as our national destiny to be in any way affected, shaped, or controlled by other nations— by any other single nation or by any congress of nations. When you have a strong sense of your national destiny, it's practically a religious mission, a divinely-ordained sequence or narrative that won't tolerate revision. You certainly don't want to let anyone else interfere with that.

Shattered dreams

YOU HAVE to go back to the founding colonies in New England to understand the persistence of that belief in God lying, standing, or sitting just behind this, that, and every other political and social or political act. American objections to and mistrust of international organizations like the League of Nations and the United Nations are connected to the fact that in our minds we already have all the partnership we need through our special relationship with God. And indeed the objections and mistrust come more from the religious right than the secular left, and they come from rural America—the South and the Midwest—more than from the East and Northeast or the coast of California, because those are the more religious regions, and from their point of view there is an antireligious taint to these international organizations.

And I guess it would not be unfair to say that American diplomacy just after World War I was instrumental in laying the groundwork for the emerging world conflict, the rise of Nazism, and the inevitability of World War II. It's so easy to sit here and look back fifty or seventy-five years and say they should have known. It's a cheap game to play, and I'd rather not do that. But as I said, Wilson and others started out on that path for reasons of state and with a mix of motives. They were trying to be practical. But some of it was psychological, some of it was imagistic—how they perceived other peoples' roles, how they perceived their own roles. And that blend is what always drives people's political actions. It's all driven by a blend or a braid of motives, never by one single motive. Which means that things didn't have to happen they way they did. The aftermath of World War I didn't have to lay the foundation for the start of World War II. It's true for individuals, and it's true for nations as well. We never do anything for one single reason. And as individuals we're rarely conscious of most of the reasons behind our behavior.

In the presidential administrations of Harding and
Coolidge and Hoover in the years leading up to the
Crash of 1929, it was felt that what was good for business
was good for America. Pure and simple. No apologies
needed. Those administrations worked hand-in-glove
with American businesses. That was a reckless, enriching
period for a whole class of people. It was a bubble economy, however, and with the Crash of 1929, the bubble
burst. All those fortunes that were based on speculation
disappeared overnight, and all the people whose jobs
and livelihoods depended on the continuing expansion
of that bubble were out of work. Mortgages were called,
loans were called. It was a society running on debt and
inflation and speculation. It all came crashing to a halt,
and there was enormous suffering as a result. The
images of the suicides of the Wall Street brokers—
investors and presidents of corporations leaping off
skyscrapers into the streets—while quite vivid, don't
really describe the pain and suffering and loss of a
much larger class of Americans, mainly the working class.

As factories shut down, banks called their loans in,
and family farms and homes were taken over. You
began to see images of that transition in movies by the
late 1930s. I mentioned earlier how in the 1930s, with
Roosevelt, there was a dramatic shift in values and
political ideology. Because the number of people who

couldn't care for themselves was so vast, there was no other place to turn than to the government. For the first time a majority of Americans came to believe that it was the government's responsibility to care for the poor and the elderly and the sick—those who couldn't care for themselves. During that period, from 1932 to World War II, there was a dramatic and historically significant shift in values in America that was forced upon us and made us a better nation and a better people.

We've always had a boom-and-bust economy. There have been booms followed by depressions approximately every thirty years going right back to the early nineteeth century, largely because our capitalist economy is based on speculation and borrowing, on optimistic anticipation of return and growth and expansion. That's the kind of capitalist economy that evolved here. It's a free-wheeling, barely controlled, speculative economy. And in the 1920s the scale simply grew too great for the system to recover when it got roughed up, and so it quickly fell apart. There are now certain guidelines and controls, put in place in the 1930s, which are designed to keep speculative growth of the economy under some restriction. So they claim. But one wonders if, in fact, it's true—that a depression like that, a crash like that, can't occur again. I'm not so sure it's true, especially when so much of our economy today is based on money that's been loaned to the US by the Chinese and by European investors, those loans passed on to the average wage-earner. We're carrying an incredibly huge debt as a nation, and if someone starts calling in that debt, if the world starts using euros instead of dollars as the basis of the oil economy, for instance, if petro-euros are used instead of petro-dollars, the American foreign debt is going to be called, and the economy may indeed crash again.

So the possibility of a crash is still there, I believe. But it was there right from the beginning of the existence of a national economy, at least from the 1820s, let's say, the time of the creation of the National Bank under Andrew Jackson, and then remained essentially unchanged into the twentieth century. This boom-and-bust economic structure has been operating at warp speed, all through the 1980s—the boom of the '80s followed by a dip in the '90s into the Bush *pere* years, booming again in the Clinton years, and deflating again during the Bush *fils* years. That's the kind of economy we've inherited from the nineteenth century, so I don't think it's something that appeared in the 1920s, but rather was already shaped early on and wasn't able to flex or shift to meet changing demands. A certain awareness of its fragility appeared in the 1930s, a consciousness of the dangers of the boom-and-bust economy. The Roosevelt administration glimpsed the implications across the board, especially with regard to the poor and the middle class, and how vulnerable they were to it. That consciousness changed our social values and our understanding of political and government structures and responsibilities.

⁂

HOW DOES all this affect the American Dream? There was in fact great confusion about the American Dream in the 1930s, because it no longer seemed possible for a man or a woman to rise in wealth, to rise up out of the working class into the middle class and beyond. For the first time, that ascent started to look like a very dim possibility at best. You saw it reflected in the movies in some ways, with the gangster-as-hero, with sympathetic portraits of gangsters played by stars like Humphrey Bogart and James Cagney and Edward G. Robinson and so on. It would be hard to imagine those types of heroes in movies prior to the Depression. In the 1920s or earlier, there weren't any Robin Hood figures robbing the rich to help the poor. The early movie heroes weren't that kind of outlaw. Instead, we got glamorous and romantic pirates, as played by Errol Flynn in *Captain Blood*. We got down-and-out gangsters, killers, snarling tough guys. Antisocial figures, really bad guys, but sympathetically portrayed. And for the first time they're at the center of American movies, and at the center of American novels, too. The noir films are very closely related to the kind of noir novels that were being written at that time by Dashiell Hammett and others. It's interesting to think about them as a possible reaction to the demise of, or the fading power of, the American Dream.

In the noir film, the whole narrative sequence, the scenery, and the sets all contrived to make the literal darkness onto which the story was projected, the view of the city as a threatening, dark environment: nothing optimistic in the imagery there. Then, at the center of the story, the violent antisocial type appears as the hero, the morally corrupted detective. Think of Bogart in *The Maltese Falcon*, and dozens of other movies like that. They were men who were morally unstable, but not morally unsure; they had what today we would call low self-esteem, and yet were piercingly clear about the morality or lack thereof of their actions. They were compromised in some way and saw themselves as compromised. In this way they were expressive of a period, the 1930s, when moral certitudes—when all certitudes—were under threat. And the noir films in some ways were a response to that.

Generally, prior to that point in American history, I think Americans felt they were perennially at the beginning of a great and clearly lit future. But with the Depression, sudden disillusionment set in—not just disappointment, but a profound challenge to our most basic belief system. And in some ways Franklin

Roosevelt was the perfect president for that moment, because he could reinvigorate that old vision of the City on a Hill and of a nation that was at the beginning of a great history, rather than at the end of one. He was able, I think, to forestall a lot of that confusion and despair.

Nonetheless, we see that confusion and despair reflected in the noir genre in an extraordinary way. As in almost every case of equal-and-opposite responses to trauma, the trauma of the Depression produced one response in the noir film, but on the Left, the Depression also gave rise to the figure of the heroic worker. Of course there was the long-running tradition of Proletarian fiction, with Theodore Dreiser and John Dos Passos, back to Stephen Crane and others, but this was more of an anti-heroic tradition. In the 1930s you got the heroic worker figure for the first time in American film, in American fiction, and in American intellectual life, with a neo-Marxist or even an overtly Marxist perspective on the worker, a romanticizing of the worker. And indeed this proved to be the only time in American history from the beginning to the present when American intellectuals and artists, novelists and filmmakers, were seriously engaged with Marxist ideas and a dialectical view of history. Even in the 1960s they never again reached that point, unless perhaps in a very parochial way on college campuses. There were some individuals, like Herbert Marcuse and so forth, who were prominent on the Left in the 1960s, but intellectuals were generally were no longer universally of the Left. Opposition to the status quo was by then single-issue opposition, against the Vietnam War, for instance, or racial segregation, rather than in systemic opposition to the society as a whole, Communism versus Capitalism and so on, whereas in the 1930s, across the board, intellectuals, artists, filmmakers, and academics were by and large committed to a Marxist point of view. And that was an extraordinary blip in the history of American art and thought and politics.

You had two kinds of responses to that diminished dream. One was the sympathetic portrayal of the outlaw, real outlaws regarded in the press and across the country as heroic figures, like Willy Sutton, the bank robber, or John Dillinger, or Bonnie and Clyde Barrow. Killers and thieves regarded as heroic figures. And of course the films reflected that. And there was the other response to the diminished dream, which was the response of the Left. For the first time in the United States, intellectuals, serious artists, filmmakers, novelists, and so on, had more than a casual flirtation with Marxism and the radical Left. For the first time, capitalism was seen as a failed system, especially by intellectuals. It was no longer unfashionable for intellectuals and artists to be politically engaged. John Ford's movie *The Grapes of Wrath* (1940) came at the end of this period, based on John Steinbeck's 1939 novel by the same name, and you could say it was the culmination of this response to the economic chaos and suffering that the Depression had brought on.

I think these were two equal and opposite responses to the same historical phenomenon. The noir film, gangsters as heroes, antisocial figures, and outlaws as heroes on the one hand, and workers as heroes and the poor and suffering as heroes on the other. It's a really interesting and linked response to the same phenomenon.

THE GREAT DICTATOR,
1940

THE DARK SIDE
ONLY GETS DARKER

AMERICANS WERE not on the whole concerned about the rise of Nazism in the period leading up to the war, or even at first during the war, the period of the late 1930s through to 1941. I spoke earlier of the prevailing view of Germany in the United States going all the way back to the late nineteeth century, how Germany was viewed as a kind of natural sibling to the US, along with England, nearly as close as that; whereas France was viewed more as a cousin than a sibling. And I described how this had to do with Germany being a northern, Protestant, Anglo-Saxon country, whereas

France was somehow seen as Mediterranean, Roman Catholic, Latin, and greatly different therefore from us, and that there might be racist tints to that, a sense that we white, Anglo-Saxon, Northern European, Protestant nations had to stick together! So I don't think what was happening in Germany in the 1930s was as frightening to the US as it would have been had it happened elsewhere, because we trusted them a little more. Also, most of the victims so far seemed to be Jews, and no way was the US going to come to the defense of Jews at that time. Especially if it was going to cost us money. The other thing was our sense simply of the physical distance between the drama being played out across Europe and ourselves. Remember that the distance across the Atlantic Ocean was far, far greater then than it is now. The preferred means of transportation was still an ocean liner rather than a plane, and so it was a question of weeks of travel, not hours. It wasn't hard in those years leading into the war for Americans to say, This doesn't concern us.

What we're talking about here, of course, isn't how Europeans actually *were*, but how Americans imagined them to be, and what distinctions Americans made between the French and the Germans, English and Irish, Spanish, Italians, and so forth. We did make distinctions, and they weren't based much on reality. They were based on mythology, on how we imagined ourselves and other countries over generations, and on our limited experience of various countries. We'd had greater exposure to the English than to other Europeans, from our shared language, if nothing else. There's greater familiarity and comfort when two nations share a language or a religion, and until recent years we believed that we shared both a language and an essentially Protestant Christian religion with England—not Ireland, however—and shared that same religion with Germany.

If language and religion were factors at play in our dealings with European nations in the late 1930s, so was race. Since we imagined ourselves as a white nation—we were not a white nation and never have been, of course, yet we have always imagined ourselves as one—we engaged with the Anglo-Saxon countries more comfortably than with others, even those that were also nominally white. These were superstitions, prejudices, and stereotypes, but that's how the human imagination functions. Superstitions, prejudices, stereotypes—mythologies, in other words—are its lifeblood.

The war in Asia, with Japan, was generated by the attack on Pearl Harbor, which was perceived very similarly to how, today, we perceive September 11—as an indefensible act justifying an all-out counterattack. The war against Germany was caused by a somewhat different sequence of events, and I think the United States was slow to intervene for various reasons. As I've said, it was easier to rationalize and justify Germany's behavior in the 1930s, even the rise of Nazism. There were a great many Americans who were very sympathetic towards Nazism.

Philip Roth published a successful novel acknowledging the historical fact that there were so many Americans who were pro-Nazi in the 1930s that, if Charles Lindbergh had run, we might have elected a pro-Nazi president. These were not just German-Americans who'd recently crossed the border in order to pursue the American Dream. We're talking about Charles Lindbergh, Henry Ford, William Randolph Hearst, Joseph Kennedy—very influential Americans with large followings. And one doesn't have to look very far from home to find it. My parents were of that generation, and I would say that my parents—who were decent, hard-working people, but not very politically sophisticated or educated—saw nothing particularly wrong with the rise of Nazism, nothing threatening in any way. I'd say they were average American voters—working people, Christians, Scots-Irish, not German—typical of their generation in many ways. All this made it very difficult to get the United States to go to war against Germany before being directly attacked by Japan.

Contrary to what many people think today, Hollywood directors and actors weren't quick to support the war effort. There was instead a desire to continue with business as usual and stay out of the war. They thought, What's that got to do with us? It's way over there in Europe. The film industry in the early 1940s was slow to react. Only in the later years of the war did they come up with a commitment to help fight it—and that was induced largely by the federal government in Washington going to the studios and saying that they needed to contribute to the war effort; they needed to make films that would inspire patriotism and demonize the Germans, demonize the Japanese, and so forth. Hollywood turned American soldiers and pilots into heroic figures for us. Films in the 1940s, starting around 1943, in some cases used actual war heroes like Audie Murphy, a Medal of Honor winner. *Sergeant York* and films like that turned real heroes into movie heroes. So, yes, the movie industry put on the uniform, but belatedly. And then it forgot to take it off.

Charlie Chaplin, with *The Great Dictator* in particular, was a special case. But Chaplin wasn't American. He was English. He was also a man of the Left, and he was very unpopular for it. *The Great Dictator* became a classic film, but it never had popular success. At the time it was made, it was regarded as the nadir of his career. He was no longer the tramp, but the tramp was what we loved him for, not for being the director of *The Great Dictator*. Making *The Great Dictator* was courageous, especially because it wasn't motivated by popular opinion. Using the most popular medium without seeking the endorsement of the audience is always courageous and difficult, and it often destroys your career. It wasn't long after that that Charlie Chaplin moved abroad. He was in a sense kicked out of the house. But his film was the exception rather than the rule.

American involvement in World War II reinforced national unity in the United States. War always does that, reinforces national identity and pride. It's tribal, after all. It affirms and asserts one's tribal identity, and that certainly occurred during World War II. American identity was affirmed in a very powerful, uniting way, particularly coming out of the Depression, when that sense of unity was not so strong.

And there was a great deal of pride in the outcome of the war, after all, with America viewing itself as the savior of Europe, to some degree rightly so. Had the Americans not intervened in Europe in 1941, it would have been lost to the Nazis. The modern history of Europe would have been very different. So there were lots of reasons for that affirmation of national identity during and after the war. That was when this notion of America being the "only light that shines in the night" really came forward. Here we'd come to save poor benighted Europe from itself! Riding to the rescue! That's how Americans viewed themselves in those years and afterwards.

At that time, in the American imagination the world was divided up between those who were free, which is to say the Americans, and the slaves of dictators, who were the Europeans. We might have looked over our shoulder and seen that our immediate close neighbors and numerous others were free as well, but we tended to see only ourselves on our hill, with the light shining brightly in the night.

That sort of black-and-white division of the world into the free and the enslaved that arose out of World War II was so seductive and powerful that it carried over into the Cold War. The Cold War simply picked up where World War II left off. And again the metaphor of those who were free and those who were enslaved, those who lived in the light and those who lived in darkness, was extended very neatly beyond 1945 to the end of the Cold War. It's a rather convenient split. Even after the end of the Cold War it's been resorted to countless times as well, almost like a sales pitch that the older generation of salesmen has told you will work every time.

They're not wrong. You see it today with George Bush's rationalization of the war in Iraq and throughout his policies, particularly in the Middle East. To save the world from itself. This refrain reappears every now and then, but not with the kind of intensity and ease as it did for the colonial powers in the nineteeth and twentieth centuries. That missionary zeal of saving the poor benighted man and woman sitting in the darkness from themselves has not been a consistent American response to the rest of the world. More often than not, we've been comfortable with our isolation. It's a natural fallback position for Americans.

⌘

THE PERIOD we're going through right now in the US, in terms of Iraq and the Middle East particularly, in many ways isn't an aberrant period at all. It's typical of America's view of our proper relationship with the rest of the world. Not even the intensity of our involvement is aberrant. Look at Panama, at Vietnam, at Korea. Or, in the nineteeth century, at the Philippines, at Cuba. We are and historically have been very involved in other parts of the world, exploiting people and lands as much as any other colonial power, in Asian, African and South American countries. But in the American imagination we're only doing that to avoid leaving them to their own terrible troubles. So there's a conflict between the reality of the nineteeth century—between the nature of our involvement with Mexico, the Caribbean, Liberia, West Africa, and later our involvement in the Philippines and in Asia in the earlier twentieth century—and the rhetoric and imagery we use to describe that involvement. So much of American violence arises because of the conflict between the reality of our lives and the perception of our lives, the way we imagine ourselves. This goes back to the early colonists in New England and Virginia and the Carolinas, who were basically committing a kind of genocide against the native people, but claimed they were saving them for Civilization, Christianity, and Capitalism. In fact they were killing them and stealing their land, but they never looked at it that way. So there was a huge conflict between what they said they were doing and what they were actually doing. And that kind of conflict in any human being, in any people, makes for a predictable, explosive violence. D. H. Lawrence said, "The essential American soul is hard, isolate, stoic, and a killer." He was pointing at the consequences of the American split between perception of self and reality. The killer is someone who would rather take a life than have to resolve that conflict between self-perception and reality.

TOWN MILITIA,
MARTINTOWN,
ALABAMA, CA. 1925

THE SHIFTING CENTER

THE MARSHALL Plan and overall US policy with regard to Europe after the war was shaped to an extraordinary degree by the Cold War, that is, by our fear of the Soviets around the world. The focus was most clearly on Europe by the late 1940s and into the '50s and then expanded from there as expanding Soviet influence became America's obsession. It was the McCarthy period in the United States. Paranoia and fear of Soviet expansion drove most of our foreign policy.

The Marshall Plan wasn't idealistic, although that's how it was sold to the American people who had to pay for it. American taxpayers paid for the Marshall Plan, just as they paid for the gigantic build-up of our military after World War II, a full-scale embrace of militarism that continued into the 1950s and beyond. In order to justify the expense that was coming out of the pockets of all Americans, you had to make people afraid, and the only thing handy was the Communist menace. Having divided the world neatly into the free and the enslaved during World War II, it wasn't a big jump to continue to divide the world into the free and the enslaved in the next few decades either. The battle lines moved to Eastern Europe and the Congo and Southeast Asia and Israel, and the planet turned half dark, half shining.

At the same time, the center of the cultural world was moving from Paris to New York. American jazz was internationally recognized as arguably the first new twentieth-century art form. American movies became the dominant mode of popular filmmaking. American painting, the New York School, replaced Paris. It looked like art but was by and large a matter of economics. The money to buy those paintings was now for the first time available in New York; the money to finance those movies was available in the US. And it was not available in Western Europe. The economic engine of the United States was at full throttle, and I think that's what made it possible for the center of modern culture to shift from Paris and London to New York and Los Angeles in the 1950s. Follow the money, as they say.

Of course the cultural conversation continued to flow back and forth. There were fresh and continuing challenges to American dominance, and they usually depended upon economics. France in the 1960s was moving economically in a direction where it could finance and distribute films, and there were filmmakers in France to challenge the Hollywood films. But then very quickly the young American filmmakers—Martin Scorsese, Francis Ford Coppola, and that whole group of young turks—learned from the French New Wave film- makers and absorbed their influence and replaced it with their own. But whatever back-and-forth there has been over the years, it's almost always been shaped by financial factors. For a brief period Germany became the center of painting, because they were able to afford to buy and house those grand paintings of the 1970s and '80s. Now Americans are buying those paintings again. There are unavoidable, direct links between economics and culture, especially when we're talking about those aspects of culture that are expensive to produce—films, public music, theater—or to own, like paintings and sculpture.

It wasn't necessarily a reflection of the quality of the work so much as it was a reflection of the prestige of the culture itself. Following World War II and in the 1950s, American values and institutions enjoyed high prestige in Europe. And it really wasn't until the Vietnam War—the late 1960s, early '70s—that Europeans began to seriously question American values. We were blessed during the 1950s and '60s to be admired by Europeans. I think we began to look a bit more cursed in the late '60s, early '70s, with the Vietnam War and the Europeans' perception of the continuing racism in the United States. Then we saw a shift in Europe away from the prestige of American filmmakers and of American artists. America began to look more threatening to the Europeans. It was in this period that the French started to protect their film industry against the invasion of American films, which had begun to look like a threat to them economically and culturally. So they started to protect themselves against the expansion of American culture, and consumerism generally, and American economic control. But even so, during the period between the 1950s until the early '70s, America looked pretty good to Europeans.

The economic power that was being exerted by the Americans, together with our dominance in culture and what I think the Europeans perceived as our political stupidity and our neurotic fixation on the Communist threat, began to create a negative preponderance of facts that made us look threatening in the European imagination. Once Europeans began to see some of our faults, they found we had many others. They noticed our racism, not just in the South but across the United States. And they saw poverty, in Appalachia and also in the inner cities of New York,

Detroit, Philadelphia, and other places. The turmoil and brutality that erupted in the late 1960s and early '70s, with the assassinations of Kennedy, Martin Luther King, and Malcolm X, and the urban riots—that whole sequence of events altered the European perception of America in a significant way. Where before we had looked to them like the golden child, we now began to take on a somewhat different appearance. The United States now looked like a bully, out of control, violent, angry, short-sighted. No longer were we the brilliant innocent.

THAT YOU can make something and sell it everywhere, everywhere on the planet, turn it into something everyone desperately wants, would be one way of describing the American reality, the one that has grown out of the one strand of the American Dream that was the dream of wealth accumulation, the one we said was the least transformative of the three strands of the American Dream, the strand that leads back to old Europe, except that now the crown heads can be anywhere or nowhere. It is the modern version of the dream of Conquest. Finally America conquers the world simply by selling material goods to every single person across the globe with money to spend.

That was Henry Ford's dream, wasn't it? Going all the way back to the Model T and the Model A, the first assembly line designs, his dream was to create cars that would be sold across the planet, across all barriers, classes, languages, national borders. That's the same for McDonald's, the same for Starbucks, where the least transformative, easiest-to-access form of the American Dream is manufactured. It's about making the one American product that everyone wants. And it's not just about dollars either, although of course selling and making money is very much the point. But McDonald's and Starbucks and, of course, Coca-Cola are also about being loved and admired by the world simply for being themselves. That Coke bottle is a great metaphor for the true apotheosis of the American Dream. What a dream! There's some kind of blissful stupidity in that impulse. If people just try Coca-Cola, they'll love me! They'll love America! If they just try a Big Mac, they'll love America. If they just try Disney World, they'll love America. If the Iraqis try democracy, they'll love America.

Well, yes, we might be making a little money on the side, but that's not the point, we say. The real point of the soft drinks, fast food, and entertainment is to show you, show the world, how good these things are that we make, show you how much you can love them and, by extension, us.

WHEN I spoke earlier of the Cold War, I think I left out something important, which was the effect of the Cold War on Europe. When you divided the world in half, as we did during the Cold War, Europe itself was halved. Eastern Europe became part of the dark half and Western Europe became part of the sunlit half, and the leadership of the sunlit half economically and militarily was generated by the United States. So during the Cold War, NATO became the creature of the United States and American arms manufacturers. Even though France and England had nuclear weapons, the United States was regarded as the primary custodian and manufacturer of both nuclear and conventional weapons. I think that political and military factors had a great deal to do with the shifting of military and cultural allegiance from Europe to the United States in the postwar years, in particular the 1950s and '60s when the Cold War was at its most intense. And I don't think it had as much to do at that time with marketing. Later in the 1980s, and certainly at an accelerated rate in the 1990s, and now, with the globalization of the economy, it has come to have everything to do with marketing.

The technological developments that came about in the 1980s changed the means and ways and techniques of outsourcing, in manufacturing as well as in the service economy, and in inventory control. These developments shifted marketing techniques and controls in a radical way in the '80s, and we haven't really begun to perceive the implications of that. Maybe there are some filmmakers out there who are putting it together, in Europe and in the United States. Maybe novelists and writers are beginning to sort out the implications of these huge economic and technological changes. Most aren't really aware of the scale of these differences, despite the fact that they have far-reaching implications, and will for many, many years, for generations.

One in three American children between the ages of eight and eighteen has a TV set in his or her own bedroom. American teenagers watch TV three hours a day. These are recent statistics from *The New York Times*. If, as a child, you have a television set in your bedroom, and you watch three hours of television a day, this has to have an effect on your perception of yourself, of reality, and of the larger world. So when you speak of younger Americans you're talking about people whose sense of reality is determined largely by a version that is at best highly filtered and at worst completely distorted. An unstated fact in those statistics is that one-third of the time that they're watching television, they're really watching advertisements for consumer goods, for products. So their minds are being organized around a need for these products. Their brains are being altered.

We know that the brain adapts to sensory input and chemically alters itself to accommodate that input in some way. So we know that's happening, and it's happening worldwide, most particularly in the United States itself and increasingly in the rest of the so-called Western world. It's useful to remember that it was during the 1950s that television was introduced into the daily life of Americans. What really happened was this: we allowed the salesman into the sanctity of the home. Because programming on television exists solely in order to sell products, television is a salesman, pure and simple. Advertising doesn't exist in order to get programs on television; it's the other way around. Programs exist in order to get consumer products advertised on television. And in the 1950s we let the salesman into the home. We started with the salesman in the living room. Then a few years later the salesman became a babysitter for the children. And now that salesman is in the bedroom with those children for three hours a day. So we've basically turned our children over to the purveyors of consumerism—the manufacturers and purveyors of sneakers, of clothing, toys, video games, junk food, and eventually, of course, of beer and liquor, drugs, and automobiles.

We've done something that has never been done. As a species we have been required to protect the young, because it takes a long time for the human child to become an adult human, longer than any other species, all in order to learn how to deal with human socialization. In ancient times, as the species evolved, we protected the young first from the weather, from the saber-toothed tigers, from the amoral forces of the universe, protected them until they were able to protect themselves. In the modern era the amoral forces of the universe are primarily economic. Thus we have all those jokes about keeping the salesman out of the house, slamming the door on the salesman's foot. This is really about protecting the young and the vulnerable, those who can't distinguish between advertisement and reality. Those jokes and cartoons implied a serious challenge by the salesman to the sanctity of the home. But when we brought the television into the home, we basically brought the salesman into the home. We brought the saber-toothed tiger into the cave and said, *Make yourself comfortable by the fire.* And now we leave the salesman babysitting the children while we step out the door and go off to work at McDonald's and Wal-Mart.

It's a very dangerous situation. We've colonized our own children. Having run out of people on the planet to colonize, run out of people who can't distinguish between beads and trinkets and something of value, having found ourselves no longer able to swap some beads and axes for Manhattan Island, we've ended up colonizing our own children. We're now engaged in a process of auto-colonization. The old sow is eating its own farrow.

We've dismantled that City on the Hill that was largely spiritual and replaced it with El Dorado, the

fantasized City of Gold. We've become the conquista-
dors of our own suburbs. Actually we've done it all while
claiming not to know what it is that we've done. It is
very possibly the end of the Republic. We're seeing
something different take place now, something alto-
gether new on this planet—a fascist plutocracy presid-
ing over a world population of disenfranchised and
distracted consumers and would-be consumers.

THE SIEGE, 1998

WHAT FOR, WHERE TO

THERE IS a statement attributed to me: "We became a dreamer of homicides." What I originally said was translated into French, then translated back again, like this entire text, and I think what I said originally was, "We became a nation of homicidal dreamers, murderous dreamers." I was trying to point indirectly to that age-old conflict between our material goals and our spiritual justifications that lie at the heart of the American Dream, and also now at the heart of American history. That conflict has made us murderers over and over again. Thus the true American is a killer. The true

American is a cynical, materialistic grabber on the one hand, reaching for gold, yet he has an idealistic, even religious, sense of mission. When you tell yourself that big a lie and you call it a dream, you're going to end up committing acts of violence. It's the nature of human psychology. If it's part of our mythology as a people, then as a people we're going to act violently. And we have historically done exactly that, beginning in the sixteenth century when the Europeans first arrived off the coast of Florida, off the coast of Virginia, off the coast of New England. We were killing people and saying that we were doing it for some higher good. Not only that, we also said we were doing it for their own good!

I regard nationalism as a kind of secular religion, a substitute religion, where the state itself and one's identity as a citizen of the state takes on a religious intensity and passion. I suppose there is a lack that's highlighted by that identification. It has behind it the notion that one's identity as an American is some kind of ultimate definition of oneself and, therefore, without it one has no identity of one's own. One's citizenship isn't merely one's group identity, it's one's essential identity.

Nationalism can do that to you. It can strip you of your individuality. And in periods of strong, nationalistic fervor in the United States, it has taken on a stubbornly religious quality. I don't think this is peculiar to us, though it is something we have periodically had to deal with. One of the healthiest and most important aspects of our American system of government is the separation of religion and the state, the sharp distinction between our legal and political system on the one hand and our religious ideas and institutions on the other. One of the things this allows is great religious tolerance; but another thing it does is demystify national identity, to secularize it. To me, this is a very good idea, something much to be desired, that the framers thoughtfully included in our national idea from the beginning.

IN THE period after September 11, 2001, there was a strong surge of national ambition and fervor. There was a plethora of American flags, from bumper stickers to flags hung on the sides of houses, on storefronts, on highway overpasses. You saw American flags everywhere. Here we are now, more than six years after 9/11, and that patriotic fervor is still controlling our thinking, our basic sense of ourselves, our personal and collective identities. To me this is a frightening thing. There is nothing positive about it. I'm at one with the poet W. H. Auden, who spoke of nationalism as a sickness, a self-imposed hallucination. To make your national identity, your citizenship, your passport, a part of your essential sense of yourself is as destructive as any hallucination. When it's a mass hallucination, it's really dangerous.

The flag has become sacred. It is as sacred to Americans as the image of Mohammed is to the Muslims. We have state laws against burning the flag or defacing the flag. These laws are solutions in search of a problem, of course. But even so, every year there's an attempt to amend the Constitution to make it a criminal act to deface or burn the flag. It's treated as if the flag were one of St. Francis's fingers or a remnant of the true cross or something like that. It's ridiculous, and, what's more important, it's very dangerous. It's tribal, and it turns the flag into a fetish object. It frightens people. And it happens periodically, when nationalism raises its ugly head, and we fall to our knees and worship the state. Politicians, of course, whip that fervor up when they want to go to war and need us to make sacrifices, financial, economic, and others—let's sacrifice our children!—that otherwise we would never make. If we weren't able to have that deep blood identification with a national fantasy, we would not be willing to sacrifice our children.

Nationalism is no longer such a necessity to Europeans living adjacent to one another as part of the European Union. Centuries of dueling nationalisms and the trauma of World War I, World War II, the Spanish Civil War, and the Cold War were sufficient to disabuse most Europeans, the Balkans aside, of the virtues of nationalism, whereas here in the United States our relative isolation has allowed us to continue to nurture the impulse. We haven't had to deal with neighbors with powerful national identities. Mexico and Canada are not threatening to the United States and its national identity. Canadians are almost apologetic of theirs. Mexico has long been regarded by Americans as our poor deracinated neighbor to the South. So we haven't had to compete with the closest neighboring countries. Also the United States' experience of World War I and World War II and even the Cold War was primarily in the European theater and in Asia. We came out of those wars, particularly World War II and the Cold War, with an inflated sense of self-importance and with our national pride reinforced by those experiences.

⁂

MAYBE WE'RE more dependent upon nationalism today simply because we're a country that was invented out of many parts. We have no ancient history as a nation or a people, so perhaps our national identity is more of an artifice, and you defend an artificial identity much more aggressively than you defend an authentic identity. The Israelis are like the Americans in this way, exceedingly nationalistic and religious, and perhaps it's because their and our identities are both artificial. They have disparate parts, people arriving from all over the world, with different languages, different races, different histories, personal and otherwise, with each new arrival being transformed into a new person by their presence in a new land. That's very artificial. Not many Americans can trace their roots to someplace within these fifty states for longer than three generations. A small number can, of course, but most can't go back three or four generations without visualizing their ancestors in the old country, wherever that may be for them. They start looking around and saying, Well, yeah, they came here from Poland or Korea, India, Mexico, Africa, Italy, Germany, and so on. I just go back one generation myself. My father was Canadian, and three of my four grandparents were Canadian, so I'm a first generation American. You cling to your national identity more strongly when you have no good reason for it to exist.

It's interesting, and maybe more problematic, for the French and the Germans and Europeans generally, because the bond of language, of shared cultural assumptions and religions, is no longer sufficient to establish national identity. And I think that the increasing number of immigrants—different racially, culturally, religiously, linguistically, and so on—in France, Germany, and England, is raising these issues of national identity in an unexpected and threatening way, raising them in ways it's not in the United States, because our national identity has, from the very beginning, been a merging process in all those areas—race, religion, language, ethnicity, land of origin. We've been merging from the start. *E pluribus unum* is on our coins: "Out of many, one." So rather than having a sense of identity preceding the arrival of the immigrants, we always were a country with an inflow that was integral to who we were.

In some ways it's a model, but I don't know that it's a model Europeans can copy. I don't think you can pick up this template and say to Europeans, this is what you ought to do with your immigrant people who are becoming so numerous—7 percent, 8 percent, 10 percent—whom you seem unable to assimilate. I don't think anything from the United States that has to do with immigration can serve as a useful model for Europe, because our histories are so radically different. We began as an invention. We began as a merging, as a merged people. We are essentially a Creole nation, a mixture, and we have been that way since our very conception. And I don't think that's true of any European country. In fact I doubt it's true of any country on the planet except for the United States and possibly Canada, except that Canada does not have the same powerful sense of its own national identity. Canada is a federation, and in many ways it still views itself as an ex-colony. Look at their coins with the imprint of the British monarchy.

⌘

THE LAST thing I want to do is to predict what is going to happen. And I mean that in both senses. Both that as I approach the end of this conversational text this is the thing I want to do, the thing I want to do last. And also that it is something I'm reluctant to do at all, since it isn't as if there's enough information here to know yet what's going to happen, so in a way it's an empty exercise, a purely speculative exercise, however tempting.

I think most Americans believe that, whenever we want to, we can still withdraw back from the world to the City on the Hill; that interventionism and being involved in the rest of the world militarily, economically, and so forth, is a choice, rather than a necessity. If threatened, if the war goes sufficiently wrong in Iraq or Afghanistan, for instance, we can pull back our troops, pull back our military engagements, and do just fine on our own. I don't think that's true, but I think most Americans believe it is. Therefore, in the next presidential campaign, in 2008, the degree to which we should be involved in Iraq, militarily and economically, will be a significant question that people will be voting on. And I think that most Americans, most politicians, will argue that we don't need to be there. We don't need to be in Iraq; we don't need to be in Afghanistan; we don't need to be involved in the so-called free trade agreements we've been pushing in Europe, in Africa, in Latin America; we can take care of ourselves just fine. I see a new period of isolationism arising as a result of the war in Iraq. And the truth is, of course, that we should have thought of those choices beforehand, because undoing what we have wrought isn't as easy as we might like to think.

There was a great hue and cry a year or so ago against George Bush and the Bush administration's decision to lease our port security to a company based in the United Arab Emirates. Suddenly we were saying, What are we doing, letting our ports be guarded by companies from the UAE? Our ports here in America should be guarded by Americans! And both sides of the aisle, Democrats and Republicans alike, were arguing against the free market global economy when they said that. They found themselves against the principle that has guided us financially on the international stage for decades. But if we can outsource our service economy to India, then we have to accept the fact that there are other countries and companies that are coming to work here as well. But suddenly there was a hue and cry against it. What we're going to see over the next five to ten years is a return to the isolationism of the past, for both good and bad reasons. The perception that we cannot continue with the Iraq war, that we cannot control events the way we think we can, that the world is a more complicated place than we'd been told, well, that's a wake-up call and a good thing. But at the same time I think we're also going to be saying we don't need the rest of the world to survive—economically, diplomatically, militarily—that we can take care of ourselves just fine, thank you. And that's a bad thing.

Further, willed isolationism ignores the presence of China—economically, militarily, diplomatically, culturally. It also ignores the future potential of India. And it ignores the simple facts of technology and its impact on the world economy. But I think that nonetheless we're falling back into isolationism, and in many ways it will be harmful to us, culturally and economically. But at least we'll kill fewer people.

YOU HAVE to see the United States as the creation of a conflicting set of impulses—spiritual, ethical, and materialistic. Despite that, or perhaps because of it, we've managed in the process, by means of the American Constitution and the Declaration of Independence, to create one of the most extraordinary political organizations on the planet. Through those documents alone we have integrated those two warring impulses more usefully than through any other existing political or social institution or structure. They have served as a bridge, incredible and unprecedented, joining together in one place in two texts all our spiritual and earthly human impulses. The texts are sacred in the sense that they tie the two together. Through them it is possible to imagine a delicate balancing act that better serves both our strengths and our weaknesses. There is a tension, a dynamic tension, between them. Sometimes that conflict takes a self-destructive route, as it has since 9/11, and at other times it gets expressed as a creative impulse, and thus we feel it as a strength.

For me, everything in the American enterprise comes back down to that dualism. This indeed is what we are blessed and cursed with, a dual identity. America has been a dualistic, and thus a contradictory, enterprise from the very beginning. Today this is played out in every theater and operation in which the United States is involved, whether economic or military, diplomatic or cultural.

But there is never just one key to understanding the American character. Whichever aspect you may be looking at, there are nearly always at least two more keys hidden there. Materialist? Yes, indeed. Religious, spiritual, idealistic? Yes, indeed. It's not one or the other. It's not one dominating the other, except period-ically. It's a dialectic, an ongoing one. Our brand of democracy has lasted for almost 200 years, over two centuries. It's the oldest continuous democracy on the planet, and the reason it's lasted this long is really due to its embodying a conflict that is so destructive—and it is truly destructive—and also so creative.

Both impulses arose in Europe. The idealistic or reli-gious impulse arose in Europe and was behind the search for freedom of religion that led the settlers to New England. The search for gold, the materialist impulse, also arose in Europe. Both of them came from the mother countries. How they met and combined in the New World was the surprise, a fresh chemistry, something profoundly different from anything that had existed before. Without the Native Americans who were here before us, who greeted us and taught us necessary skills for living in this new world, we'd be more like the Europeans. Without the Africans, who were brought into this New World as the first immigrants, as slaves for several hundred years and then as second-class citizens for another hundred years, we'd be more like the Europeans. When I speak of America as a Creole nation, I am not speaking only of the waves of immigrants that came after, but of the very seed of us that was and has always been in the mixture. So it is both ironic and revealing that our national obsession, looking outward and away, has always been a racial obsession, since in my view the seed inside us was always closer to that complex brew than it ever was to the picture we had of ourselves as white, Anglo-Saxon, Protestant Northern Europeans.

When I look at us Americans, I feel I see people I know well. We aren't mixed together in a "melting pot." Nor do we live behind walls to protect ourselves from outsiders, since our own identity as outsiders is deeply imbedded within us. Instead I begin by recognizing that the way this country was formed, and the way it is

still coming into being, is a powerful, combustible combination of energies. We would do well to recognize
that we haven't yet finished making ourselves, and that
we can still take mindful control of that process. Our
American history is taking us somewhere. We just don't
know where yet.

We're sitting here today in Saratoga, New York.
York, of course, is an English name. But Saratoga is an
Iroquois Indian word. Originally, this place was called
Sarachtoque, which means "hillside of a great river," or
"place of the swift water." Half the place names in New
York are Indian names. Ours is a true Creole culture,
and it would be very interesting for us and for the world
around us if one day we came around to seeing ourselves in all our component parts, acknowledging
finally the only identity that's ours.